THE MARSHALL CAVENDISH
☆ ☆ ☆ ILLUSTRATED ☆ ☆ ☆
ENCYCLOPEDIA OF
WORLD WAR II

Based on the original text by
Lieutenant Colonel Eddy Bauer

CONSULTANT EDITOR

Brigadier General James L. Collins, Jr., U.S.A.

CHIEF OF MILITARY HISTORY,
DEPARTMENT OF THE ARMY

MARSHALL CAVENDISH CORPORATION/NEW YORK

CONTENTS

Editorial Director: Brian Innes
Editor-in-chief; Brigadier Peter Young, D.S.O., M.C., M.A.
Managing Editor: Richard Humble
Editor: Christopher Chant
Art Editor: Jim Bridge

CHAPTER 22

FRANCE: the fatal decision

In the event of France agreeing to a separate armistice, despite the Anglo-French agreement of March 28, what would be the attitude of Britain and her Government–in other words, of Churchill?

When he left the Château du Muguet on June 12, Churchill had taken the Commander-in-Chief of the French Navy aside and had said to him privately, according to Churchill's own account in *The Second World War:* "Darlan, you must never let them get the French Fleet."

Was Churchill already anticipating that France would ignore his urgings that she continue resistance? To say this is so is not reading too much into his words; later, writing on the same subject to President Roosevelt, Churchill mentioned the possibility that the conditions of the Italo-French armistice might be so mild that France, in order to retain Alsace and Lorraine, would seriously consider handing over her fleet to Germany and Italy.

The fleet safeguarded

What would this mean? In capital ships alone – the epitome of naval power in 1940 – the Axis strength would be raised to 15 battleships and battle-cruisers (seven of them French), against the Royal Navy's 14. If the two German pocket-battleships were included in the reckoning, the Axis combined battle fleet would be 17 strong. Darlan, however, as Churchill recounts, "promised solemnly that he would never do so". He was quite sincere in this: on May 28 he had written to Vice-Admiral Le Luc: "Should military events result in an armistice in which the conditions would be dictated by the Germans, and should one of those conditions mean the surrender of the fleet, *I have no intention of carrying out that order.*"

If matters were to come to such a pass, Darlan suggested several courses of action, depending on whether or not Italy had entered the war and thus had a say in the armistice. But whatever the outcome, he wrote, "all warships and aircraft, all auxiliary and supply ships capable of putting to sea, are to make for the nearest British port they can reach."

AMIRAL DARLAN.

HONNEUR ET PATRIE — VALEUR ET DISCIPLINE

Entré à l'École Navale en 1899, Amiral de la Flotte en 1939 : entre ces deux dates, François DARLAN accomplit tout ce dont peut rêver un marin. Son premier embarquement le mène

Tours: the last Allied meeting

On June 13, Churchill and Lord Beaverbrook met Reynaud at Tours. The latter's Council of Ministers was not present, but met at Cangé after Reynaud's departure. This is how the afternoon began, in Benoist-Méchin's words:

"After lunch M. Baudouin accompanied

△ *Popular print of François Darlan, French Admiral. After France's collapse he came to be reviled as one of the country's Quisling leaders collaborating with the enemy–but he promised Churchill that the Germans would never lay hands on the French fleet, and he was true to his word.*

△ *Taken after one of the last dramatic meetings of the Franco-British leaders: Churchill, Sir John Dill, British Ambassador to France Sir Ronald Campbell, Labour leader Clement Attlee, and Paul Reynaud. Despite Churchill's urgings, Reynaud did not prove strong enough to overcome the "softs" who wanted to conclude an armistice and stop the fighting.*

portant meetings of these 60 days was about to be enacted."

The accounts which we have of the attitudes taken by both parties in this their last meeting before 1945 are contradictory. Churchill's statement to the House of Commons claimed that he definitely turned down Reynaud's plea that France should be released from her engagement of March 28. But was this refusal really so categorical? There are grounds for doubt, for Reynaud, testifying before the Commission of Inquiry between 1947 and 1950, claimed that such authorisation would have been granted to him without his having to ask for it, but that it would have been arranged that he would be able to retract it. To that effect he might have used General de Gaulle, sent to London that evening, as a go-between.

Withdrawal to Bordeaux

When the French Council of Ministers met at Cangé after the Anglo-French conference at Tours, the mood was sombre: "In such an atmosphere the meeting of the Council opened," wrote Reynaud in his memoirs. "Chautemps was the spokesman of his colleagues...to whom I gave... the news that Churchill was not coming...

"Here is how Georges Monnet in his deposition has retraced for the Committee of Inquiry the incident when Weygand attempted to teach the Government a lesson:

"'Campinchi was amongst the Ministers who declared most bluntly, in opposition to Weygand, their opinion that we should not lay down our arms or ask for an armistice. It was, therefore, he whom Weygand took to task by asking him: "But, M. Minister, if I had been a politician, if I had been in the Government, I would not have left Paris. I would have acted like the Roman Senators at the time when the Gauls invaded Rome. In my curule chair, I should have awaited the invader. But there has been only one occasion on which the geese have saved the Capitol!'

"Louis Rollin remembers that: 'The President of the Republic, who looked disconcerted by this attitude, was near Weygand. He clapped him on the arm in friendly fashion and said: 'But look now, General, if you follow your argument to its logical conclusion. The Government is taken prisoner, but do you really think

Mr. Churchill and the British ministers to the Prefecture. There, instead of being driven to Cangé, they were shown into a small room on the first floor that served as the Prefect's office. M. Mandel, the Minister of the Interior, had taken it over for the time being and was on the point of beginning lunch. Churchill records in his memoirs:

"'His luncheon, an attractive chicken, was uneaten on the tray before him. He was a ray of sunshine. He had a telephone in each hand, through which he was constantly giving orders and decisions.'

"M. Reynaud then arrived, followed a few minutes later by General Spears. Churchill took Spears aside and asked him what was going on. Spears swiftly brought him up to date with the situation. Baudouin, he said, was now 'doing his damnedest to persuade Reynaud to throw up the sponge'. Churchill replied that he had gathered as much: Baudouin had ruined an already inadequate meal by seasoning it with an outpouring of oily defeatism.

"It was now 3.30 pm. The conference was about to begin. Having finished his lunch, M. Mandel left the room, carrying his tray, and Reynaud replaced him at the desk.

"The British ministers and Baudouin sat in a semi-circle in front of him, in this little room in which one of the most im-

that that would do the country any good? How can a captive Government discuss either an armistice or a continuation of the war? It is no longer master of its own will . . . Come now, think it over . . .'

"The General maintained his position," Reynaud continues. "He was obdurate in his opposition to the policy which I had advocated the day before, that of liberating France with the aid of the Anglo-Saxon world.

"But after finishing his exposition Weygand left the room abruptly on the grounds that one of the Ministers – it was Mandel – had smiled."

Reynaud left the next day for Bordeaux, where the French Government was planning to base itself. His memoirs contain some details of the unhappy journey:

"At 10 o'clock in the morning on the 14th I got into my car in the Cour Renaissance of the Château de Chissay, which was to be bombed only an hour later – proof that the enemy was well informed. But for once those gentlemen were late.

"I drove towards Bordeaux, my car escorted by army motorcyclists. Every mile which carried me away from Paris, now occupied by the enemy, was agony for me. Never has a French head of government been in a situation like mine. 'The Germans are at Noyon,' Clemenceau had said. They had not been in Paris. The English had jeered at Charles VII as 'the King of Bourges'. But now, perhaps, Bourges too would fall in a few days. The entire country could soon be carved up by the tracks of the Panzer divisions.

"On the way we were stopped by a closed level crossing. Some refugees cheered me. One of them said to a gendarme: 'For once we can see a minister and wish him all the best; don't stop us.' A woman came up to me and said: 'I come from Paris. My husband's been called up. So what if Paris has been taken. Hang on! We're all with you.'

"I arrived at the Bordeaux prefecture at about 2000 hours. I walked across the courtyard, bareheaded. Many generals and politicians saluted me in silence.

"I was visited by de Gaulle who asked

▽ *Glow of victory: passing German gunners survey a lolling group of French prisoners during the Wehrmacht's decisive drive into central and southern France.*

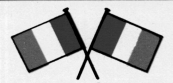

A TOUS LES FRANÇAIS

La France a perdu une bataille!
Mais la France n'a pas perdu la guerre!

Des gouvernants de rencontre ont pu capituler, cédant à la panique, oubliant l'honneur, livrant le pays à la servitude. Cependant, rien n'est perdu!

Rien n'est perdu, parce que cette guerre est une guerre mondiale. Dans l'univers libre, des forces immenses n'ont pas encore donné. Un jour, ces forces écraseront l'ennemi. Il faut que la France, ce jour-là, soit présente à la victoire. Alors, elle retrouvera sa liberté et sa grandeur. Tel est mon but, mon seul but !

Voilà pourquoi je convie tous les Francais, où qu'ils se trouvent, à s'unir à moi dans l'action, dans le sacrifice et dans l'espérance.

Notre patrie est en péril de mort.
Luttons tous pour la sauver !

VIVE LA FRANCE !

C. de Gaulle

GÉNÉRAL DE GAULLE

QUARTIER-GÉNÉRAL,
4, CARLTON GARDENS,
LONDON, S.W.1.

△ *"France has lost a battle, but France has not lost the war!" De Gaulle's famous proclamation of June 18, announcing that there was a "rebel" French government-in-exile determined to fight on, gave the British almost as many problems as it did to the Germans. Which side would be able to make the most capital out of de Gaulle? He was in London—but Hitler (opposite) was master of France. He indulged in a lightning sight-seeing trip around Paris at the crack of dawn on Sunday, June 23.*

me where he would find me again and I replied, as he says in his memoirs, 'In Algiers'. He set off for London to organise the shipping for the retreat to North Africa."

Pétain's ultimatum

On the 16th, there was a meeting of the Council of Ministers which began in the morning and finished only in the evening.

Benoist-Méchin recalls:

"M. Reynaud began by reading out President Roosevelt's reply to his appeal of June 14. M. Lebrun records that the words of the President's telegram had 'a profoundly depressing effect on the Council'.

"M. Chautemps then asked the Premier to inform his colleagues of the result of the representations that the previous night's meeting had instructed him to make to the British Government.

" 'Nothing is settled yet,' M. Reynaud answered defiantly. 'I am still waiting for Mr. Churchill's answer to the questions I put to him last evening through Sir Ronald Campbell. But what I *can* tell you is that the British Cabinet has never ratified its leader's conciliatory statements . . .'

"At this, Marshal Pétain rose to his feet.

" 'I can no longer remain in the government,' he said. 'Our armies are disintegrating more and more as time goes by. The inevitable solution has been put off all too long. I have no wish to be associated with this delay, for which the whole of France is paying.'

"These words brought utter dismay to the meeting. Everyone sensed that in these tragic hours the French were turning more and more to the Marshal. If he resigned, the Government would fall. As he made to leave the room President Lebrun burst out: 'Oh no! You are not going to do *that* to us now!'

The majority of the ministers present begged the Marshal to remain in office and continue to 'afford the government the benefit of his prestige'. The Marshal gave in but refused to sit down again."

At about 1400 hours on the 16th the British Ambassador, Sir Ronald Campbell, accompanied by General Spears, entered President Lebrun's office at Bordeaux. They brought with them a telegram defining the conditions under which the British Government would consent to France entering into negotiations for an armistice with the common enemy:

"June 16, 1940, 12.35 pm.

Our agreement forbidding separate negotiations, whether for armistice or peace, was made with the French Republic, and not with any particular French Administration or statesman. It therefore involves the honour of France. Nevertheless, *provided, but only provided, that the French Fleet is sailed forthwith for British harbours pending negotiations*, His Majesty's Government give their full consent to an enquiry by the French Government to ascertain the terms of an armistice for France. His Majesty's Government, being resolved to continue the war, wholly exclude themselves from all part in the above-mentioned inquiry concerning an armistice."

When this document was read to him, Reynaud, according to Spears, burst out:

"What a very silly thing to do, to ask that the French Fleet should go to British harbours when it is in fact at this very moment protecting Algeria and the Western Mediterranean. And you ask us to do this at the very moment you are inviting us to go to North Africa: *non, vraiment, c'est trop bête!*"

Spears recalls that Reynaud continued: "This suggestion means offering all French North African harbours to the Italian Fleet as targets . . . It is really too silly. For one thing, the French Fleet is relieving the British in the Mediterranean. To send ours away would place a fresh strain on yours."

At 1510 another message was sent out from London to be passed onto the French Government by Sir Ronald Campbell, redefining the above terms. The British Government – naturally enough – asked to be kept informed of the progress of negotiations if France should ask for an armistice. Equally naturally, the British asked for the evacuation of all Polish, Czech and Belgian troops fighting with the French Army. Campbell carried out his instruc-

REVOLUTION
NATIONALE

tions, with the result that over 24,300 Poles and nearly 5,000 Czechs were embarked for England. But only 163 Belgians left France.

The Declaration of Union

Spears was in the room when a telephone call came through for Reynaud. It was General de Gaulle in London, who proceeded to dictate, word by word, the text of a "Declaration of Franco-British Union". This document was the result of discussions between French Ambassador Corbin, Jean Monnet and René Pleven, members of the Economic Mission in London, and the British leaders. It read as follows:

"At this most fateful moment in the history of the modern world the Governments of the United Kingdom and the French Republic make this declaration of indissoluble union and unyielding resolution in their common defence of justice and freedom against subjugation to a system which reduces mankind to a life of robots and slaves.

"The two Governments declare that France and Great Britain shall no longer be two nations, but one Franco-British Union.

"The constitution of the Union will provide for joint organs of defence, foreign, financial, and economic policies.

"Every citizen of France will enjoy immediately citizenship of Great Britain; every British subject will become a citizen of France.

"Both countries will share responsibil-

ity for the repair of the devastation of war, wherever it occurs in their territories, and the resources of both shall be equally, and as one, applied to that purpose.

"During the war there shall be a single War Cabinet, and all the forces of Britain and France, whether on land, sea, or in the air, will be placed under its direction. It will govern from wherever best it can. The two Parliaments will be formally associated. The nations of the British Empire are already forming new armies. France will keep her available forces in the field, on the sea, and in the air. The Union appeals to the United States to fortify the economic resources of the Allies, and to bring her powerful material aid to the common cause.

"The Union will concentrate its whole energy against the power of the enemy, no matter where the battle may be.

"And so we shall conquer."

Reynaud heard of the proposed Union by telephone. Spears records that:

". . . the telephone rang. Reynaud took up the receiver. The next moment his eyebrows went up so far they became indistinguishable from his neatly brushed hair. 'One moment,' he said, 'I must take it down,' and grasping a sheet of foolscap on the slippery table, he began to write, using a short gold pencil with an enormous lead. He repeated each word as he wrote it, and listening I became transfixed with amazement. Reynaud was taking down in French, from de Gaulle's dictation in London, the text of the Declaration of Union proposed by the British Government. On he wrote in a frightful scrawl, getting more excited as the message unfolded. The paper skidded on the smooth surface of the table. I held it. As each sheet was covered I handed him a fresh one. His pencil gave out; I handed him mine.

"Finally he stopped and said into the telephone: 'Does he agree to this? Did Churchill give you this personally?' There was a moment's pause and now he was speaking in English. It was evident that de Gaulle had handed the receiver to Churchill, who was assuring him that the document was a decision of the Cabinet. If there were alterations, they would be merely verbal.

"Reynaud put the receiver down. He was transfigured with joy, and my old friendship for him surged out in a wave of appreciation at his response, for he was happy with a great happiness in the belief that France would now remain in the war. This was his thought as it was ours, and in those first moments this was all that

◁ In June 1940 the legendary figure of Marshal Pétain was as a beacon of hope to millions of Frenchmen. He had saved Verdun from the massive German assaults in 1916. He had nursed the French Army back to health after the shattering experiences of the spring 1917 offensive had nearly broken it. Of all the French leaders in 1940 he stood out as the man most pledged to avoid useless sacrifice. But there was another side to Pétain; as an adviser had once said to him: "You think too much about the French and not enough about France." ▽ Propaganda for the "New Order" in western Europe: the new broom sweeps corruption and profiteering out of France, and (bottom) promises a new era of prosperity for Luxembourg.

△ The train of German devastation spreads south through France: ruins at Gien on the Loire. . .
▷ △ . . . and in Orléans. Hopes of a French stand on the line of the Loire were stifled at birth. And as the spearheads of the Wehrmacht drove into southern France, the position of the French Government at Bordeaux became more and more hopeless with every hour.

the two statesmen agreed to meet at Concarneau on the following day. To the approval of General Spears, who had disapproved violently of the British concessions to the French point of view, Sir Ronald Campbell recovered the two telegrams which conflicted with the new instructions received from his Government.

Pétain takes over

The French Council of Ministers met again at 1700 hours in the Prefecture of the Gironde. But despite two addresses from Reynaud, the projected Franco-British Union was greeted far more unfavourably than it had been by Churchill the day before.

The majority of the French ministers gave an icy reception to the new plan. Was Reynaud, under the excuse that they had been cancelled, deliberately avoiding mention of the import, and even the existence, of the two telegrams which the British Ambassador had recently brought to his knowledge? Most of the ministers regarded the plan, quite simply, as a will o' the wisp, but not all of them favoured the alternative solution of an armistice concluded in defiance of the British. In fact, the proposals from London could well have led to a French counter-proposal.

But it never came. When the session was suspended Reynaud handed his resignation to President Lebrun and named Pétain as his successor. Reynaud could still hear the old Marshal declaring to the Council on June 13 that if the Government left France, he would consider it desertion, and that he himself would refuse to leave metropolitan France. He would stay with the French people to share in their miseries. "The armistice," he had concluded, "is, as I see it, the only guarantee of the survival of eternal France."

Whether or not Pétain was right, it is quite clear that Reynaud was well aware in advance of the programme which would be adopted by his successor, and that despite his own convictions he did not hesitate to step down in Pétain's favour.

The news of Reynaud's resignation reached Churchill as he was embarking on a special train for Southampton, where a destroyer was waiting to take him to Concarneau. De Gaulle heard of Reynaud's resignation in favour of Pétain as he landed at Bordeaux airport. He did not hesitate a moment about what he must do.

mattered. The sense of the generosity of the offer was overwhelming, the sincerity of the gesture completely convincing."

In his memoirs, Churchill does not hide the fact that his first reaction to the draft of the Declaration of Union was unfavourable, but that he yielded to the wave of enthusiasm which swept the members of his War Cabinet. Nevertheless, This "immense design whose implications and consequences were not in any way thought out," would, he hoped, have the advantage "of giving M. Reynaud some new fact of a vivid and stimulating nature with which to carry a majority of his Cabinet into the move to Africa and the continuance of the war".

In which he was wrong. Reynaud, certainly, remained enthusiastic about the project which Churchill had recommended to him via de Gaulle, but he still had to convince his ministers. In the meantime

"Heavy water" snatched from the Germans

On the night that Reynaud's Government fell, June 16–17, the British merchantman *Broompark* sailed from the small port of Bassens (Gironde). She had just embarked 26 containers containing the 410 pounds of "heavy water" which Frederic Joliot-Curie had earlier removed from Norway with the help of Jacques Allier of French Military Intelligence. The physicists Hans-Heinrich Halban and Lew Kowarski accompanied this precious cargo. They were under orders signed by Bichelonne, principal secretary to Armaments Minister Raoul Dautry, to write a report of the research carried out by the Collège de France, but to keep it absolutely secret. With them sailed Lord Suffolk and Berkshire, scientific liaison officer to the French Government. The groundwork and experiments carried out by Joliot-Curie (with the aim of producing an explosion as a result of atomic fission) were to be a vital link in the chain of events which led to Hiroshima.

Pétain's goal: armistice with Germany

While Pétain was waiting for his call to supreme office, he had the time to compile a list of the men from whom he would form his Government. Paul Baudouin was named as Foreign Minister, Yves Bouthillier as Finance Minister, and Camille Chautemps as Vice-President. Weygand was named as Chief of National Defence; General Colson as C.-in-C. Army, General Pujo as C.-in-C. Air Force, while Darlan retained the supreme command of the Navy. Pierre Laval was offered the post of Minister of Justice, but he turned this down: he wished to be Foreign Minister. Pétain, however, was unwilling to give Laval this post as he was trying to avoid any gesture which might be interpreted as provocative by the British.

Pétain's Government was formed at 2330 hours on June 16. It included a Marshal of France, three generals, an admiral, seven deputies, one senator, and five high-ranking civil servants, and wasted no time in carrying out its immediate pro-gramme, the conclusion of an armistice. At 0100 hours on the 17th, Baudouin asked the Spanish Ambassador to send, via Madrid, a request to the German Government for negotiations. As morning came it was realised that a similar approach must be made to Italy, and the Papal Nuncio was contacted for this task.

Some hours later the French radio was broadcasting to every home the poignant message of Marshal Pétain, announcing that the enemy had been asked to enter into discussions on how hostilities might be ended. It was a noble and dignified address, but its effect upon the fighting troops was as unfortunate as on the civilian population and the local authorities.

A few days before, Chautemps had suggested that the enemy should be sounded out by undercover means. It was a naïve idea; the German propagandists would only have trumpeted the news to the

▽ *The Germans were not slow to poke fun at the inadequacy of the Allied war effort. This cartoon, entitled "The End", depicts decadent Western democratic plutocracy as tearfully laying a wreath on a funeral pyre of smashed and useless Allied war material.*

While the politicians argued, the Battle of France continued unabated. ▷ *Artillery of the front line: a German "tank-hunting" crew.* ▽ *Artillery of the rear: long-range German artillery probes for targets behind the French line.* ▷ *As they fell back to the south the French made desperate efforts to slow down the Germans. These are two of the blown bridges on the Loire.*

world. Still more, they would have used every method at their disposal, especially pamphlets, to incite the French to stop fighting there and then.

Until the conditions of an armistice could be agreed between the French, the Germans, and the Italians, the fighting went on – along the Alps, in the Vosges, in the Maginot Line, on the Loire and in western France, bringing in more trophies for Hitler and more setbacks for Mussolini. For the sake of clarity we will follow the surrender talks at Rethondes and the Villa Incisa, and only then attempt to unravel the operations of this sixth and final week of the Battle of France.

De Gaulle flies to England

Meanwhile, however, there occurred an event which was to prove just as important as the policy of Marshal Pétain. From the aerodrome at Bordeaux-Mérignac an aircraft took off for England, carrying General de Gaulle, Reynaud's former Under-Secretary of State for War. There are several descriptions of the event, all romanticised to some extent; but this is de Gaulle's own version:

"Late in the evening I went to the hotel where Sir Ronald Campbell, the British Ambassador, was residing, and informed him of my intention to leave for London. General Spears, who came and joined in the conversation, declared that he would accompany me. I sent word to Reynaud. He made over to me 100,000 francs, on the secret funds. I begged M. de Margerie to send at once to my wife and children, who were at Carentec, the necessary passports for reaching England, which they could do by the last boat to leave Brest. On June 17th, at nine in the morning, I flew off with General Spears and Lieutenant de Courcel, in the British aeroplane which had brought me the evening before. There was nothing romantic or difficult about the departure."

Passed on without delay by Madrid, the French Government's request for armistice discussions soon reached the Germans. Hitler hastened to meet his Italian ally at Munich: the Axis leaders would have to be in full agreement between themselves if they were to prevent the defeated French from playing off one against the other.

The Italo-German conference in Munich began at the *Führerbau* in the afternoon of June 18. On the German side were

Hitler, Ribbentrop, and Keitel; Mussolini brought with him Ciano and General Roatta, Deputy Chief of the Italian General Staff. Paul Schmidt, Hitler's interpreter, was present, but his memoirs include only a few lines about these discussions. However, the transcript taken by General Roatta has survived. Two years later Ciano gave it to General Carboni, then commanding the "Friuli" Division at Livorno, saying: "Look, this is the bill of sale for the bear's skin. You can use it one day when writing the history of the war."

As the armistice conditions laid down by Hitler on June 18 were on the whole identical to those signed by the French delegation on the 22nd, they can be examined in due course. But the programme drawn up by the Italians during their journey can, according to Carboni's version, be summarised in eight extremely ambitious sections:

1. Immediate demobilisation of the French Army;
2. Immediate surrender of all the Army's weapons, of all warships, and of all aircraft;
3. Occupation of all French territory between the Alps and the Rhône, with bridgeheads on the right bank of the Rhône at Lyons, Valence, and Avignon, and the occupation of Corsica;
4. Occupation of Tunisia and of French Somaliland. Occupation of the naval bases of Algiers, Mers el Kébir and Casablanca. Beirut to become a neutral port, and Italy to have the right to occupy it;
5. Italy to have the right to occupy any part of metropolitan France or her Empire considered necessary for the conduct of operations, the maintenance of peace, or the establishment of order;
6. France to be forbidden to make any demolitions or to evacuate any railway material from the zone marked down for Italian occupation;
7. Denunciation of the Franco-British alliance. Removal of all British forces in metropolitan France and the Empire;
8. Disarmament and disbandment of all Polish, Belgian, and other foreign forces in France.

When Hitler first heard this programme, he approved of the Italian claims to occupy French territory. Joining hands in the region of Geneva, the Axis partners would hold the railway axis of Dijon-Modane, through Ambérieu and Culoz, and would completely encircle Switzerland. How-

ever, the immediate handing-over of the French fleet to the Italians seemed, to Hitler, to raise certain problems.

As he saw it, all the evidence suggested that the French would refuse to surrender their fleet. If this were demanded of them, rather than scuttle the fleet they might well prefer to see it pass into British hands, which would be a disaster for the Axis. It would be better to demand a controlled neutralisation of the French fleet, either in French or neutral ports (Spanish for preference), leaving the French with the hope that they might recover it once peace was signed. Mussolini agreed to this.

As to the rest, Mussolini believed that Hitler wanted to spare the German people from another winter of war, and was anxious not to provoke American intervention. On a question put by Ciano to Ribbentrop Hitler had commented: "You must not aim so high; you must be moderate. I hope you have no designs on Croatia and other items of the sort."

Singular moderation, one might think – but it would not prevent Hitler from demanding the annexation of Alsace, Lorraine, and the Briey basin. Moreover, Belgium would have to make several frontier rectifications in favour of the Reich, and Norway would have to submit to the permanent occupation of her main ports, as part of Germany's consolidation of her war gains so far. In Africa, the annexation of the Congo would link together all the former German colonies whose return Hitler would demand. Finally, Spain would receive a protectorate over Morocco with the exception of the ports on the Atlantic, which would go to Germany.

Mussolini had no objections to make to this programme. His own claims comprised the Department of the Maritime Alps, Corsica, Algeria, Tunisia, and French Somaliland. Once Britain was beaten, the British territories of Egypt, the Anglo-Egyptian Sudan, and British Somaliland would fall to Italy. Gibraltar would be returned to Spain, but both sides of the Strait of Gibraltar would be declared neutral territory.

But would Britain be beaten? Hitler, as Mussolini noted, had only hinted at a direct cross-Channel attack, and even this hint was extremely vague and totally hypothetical. Was Hitler thinking of playing Charlemagne without giving any more thought to Italy's interests? Ciano noted, with a certain amount of uneasiness, the considerate feelings which the majestic

edifice of the British Empire inspired in Hitler.

As far as plans for the immediate future were concerned, Keitel assured Roatta, the German Army would not slow down its pursuit; it would strike with its armoured columns at the rear of the French forces defending the Alps at the moment when they were under attack from in front by the Italian thrusts across the Little St. Bernard, the Col de la Madeleine, and along the coast. It was also agreed that the final Franco-German armistice would not come into force until the *Comando Supremo* declared that its requirements had been met. But the two negotiations would remain separate – a fact which was unlikely to be of much advantage to the Italians.

◁ *The vanquished – a dejected huddle of French prisoners*
△ *The victors – a German infantry column tramps across open country with no enemy to molest them.*

CHAPTER 23
Armistice

At 1430 hours on June 20 the French deputation left Bordeaux. General Huntziger presided; the former Ambassador to Poland, Léon Noël, was attached as political adviser; Vice-Admiral Le Luc and General Bergeret represented the Navy and the Air Force respectively. The deputation was basically an exploratory one; it was to find out what the German terms were and try to improve on them, but to sign nothing without an express order from the French Government. To the question of what should be done if the Germans made the surrender of the French fleet a *sine qua non* for the granting of an armistice, Admiral Darlan, Noël states, "replied categorically that orders had been given that if this demand were made, whatever the Government's decision, our warships would not fall into the hands of the Germans".

At 1530 hours on the following day General von Tippelskirch, head of the Führer's G.H.Q. staff, led the French delegates into Marshal Foch's railway carriage, which the Germans had moved to the clearing at Rethondes. There they found, standing at the Nazi salute, Hitler, Ribbentrop, Hess, Göring, Keitel, and Raeder. When everyone had taken his place, Hitler gestured to Keitel to proceed. In a thundering voice, Keitel read out a preamble in which lies were masked by a few chivalrous phrases; then, "with a brusque gesture, Hitler handed each of the French delegates a copy of the armistice terms and left the carriage without having said a word. "There was nothing imposing," recalled Noël, "in either his attitude or his gesture: huddled, tired-looking, sullen, wearing a cap too big for him surrounded by a maroon velvet band; his traits, his hands, were vulgar and expressionless."

No discussion worthy of the name followed Hitler's exit, for at the first attempt at modification made by Huntziger, Keitel exclaimed that his task was to comment on the articles of the convention prepared by the Führer, not to discuss them. But on Noël's calm insistence Keitel agreed to put the French deputation in telephone communication with the Government at Bordeaux.

In the clearing at Rethondes on June 22, 1940, the Nazi leaders preside over the greatest international triumph in German history: the surrender of France.
◁ *Hitler and Göring.*
△ *Himmler and Ribbentrop.*

The French and German delegates met twice. With only a few exceptions, the Germans refused to consider any modification to the text of the 24 articles, which were to be accepted as they stood. After a vehement protest by General Bergeret, Keitel, after obtaining Göring's approval, agreed to spare the French from having to hand over their military aircraft as laid down in Article 6. The aircraft would merely be disarmed and put in safe-keeping under German control.

But Article 8 was crucial. It dealt with the French fleet, and its terms are worth quoting in full:

"Article 8. The French battle fleet – apart from the portion which is to be left at the disposition of the French Government for safeguarding France's interests in her colonial Empire – will be collected in ports which have still to be determined, to be decommissioned and disarmed under the control of Germany or Italy respectively.

"The designation of these ports will be made according to the peacetime home ports of the ships. The German Government solemnly declares to the French Government that it has no intention during the war of making effective use of the French warships stationed in ports under German control, with the exception of

ips needed for coastal patrolling and inesweeping.

"Moreover, the German Government eclares, solemnly and formally, that it as no intention of making further claims n the French battle fleet after the conlusion of peace. With the exception of hat part of the French fleet still to be etermined which will be entrusted with he security of France's interests in her olonial Empire, all warships outside rench territorial waters are to be recalled o France."

In the face of these requirements Huntger countered by pointing out the risk hat the French warships forced to return o the German-occupied ports of Cherourg, Brest, and Lorient could well be ombed and destroyed by the R.A.F. He roposed instead that their decommissiong and disarmament should be carried ut in North African naval bases. In fact, Iuntziger was trying to prevent the most owerful units in the French battle fleet – *Dunkerque* and *Strasbourg* at Mers el Kébir, *Jean Bart* at Casablanca, and *Richelieu* at Dakar – from being put at the mercy of the Germans.

Obviously, Keitel was not taken in by his. But although he refused emphatically o make the least modification to the basic rovisions of Article 8, he nevertheless pointed out to Huntziger that the German text – which would be definitive – did not use the word *müssen* ("must"), which implied a binding imperative, but *sollen* ("should"), a more vague expression of an obligation in principle. This would make possible a solution nearer to the wishes of the Bordeaux Government.

But at 1834 hours on June 22 (German time) the French deputation was given a brutal ultimatum. If Huntziger did not sign the document in front of him within one hour, the order would be given for him to be sent back behind the firing-line and the war would continue. With the dagger at his throat, Huntziger signed.

Next morning the French delegates left Paris for Rome, aboard three aircraft put at their disposal by the Luftwaffe.

The Jackal's feast

At Bordeaux, naturally, the Government still had no way of knowing that Mussolini had finally been converted to Hitler's point of view concerning the neutralisation of the French fleet. Because of this, Darlan, with Pétain's approval, sent the following telegram to Admirals Esteval, Duplat, and Gensoul at 1810 of June 22:

◁ *Hitler's reaction to the news of the French surrender: his notorious "jig of joy". His instinctive reaction was hardly inexcusable: excited gestures an exultant stamp of the foot.*
△ *Hitler, surrounded by the armed forces' chiefs and his deputy – Brauchitsch, Raeder, Hess, Göring, and Keitel – paces solemnly towards the railway carriage in which Marshal Foch accepted the German surrender in 1918. "I observed his face." wrote the eye-witness William Shirer, "It was grave, solemn, yet brimming with revenge. There was also in it, as in his springy step, a note of the triumphant conqueror, the defier of the world. There was something else, difficult to describe, in his expression, a sort of scornful, inner joy at being present at this great reversal of fate – a reversal he himself had wrought."*

△ *The French deputation arrives in the clearing at Rethondes: Huntziger, Léon Noël (partially obscured by a German officer), Admiral Le Luc, and General Bergeret.* ▷ *After the departure of Hitler the armistice conference gets down to the discussion of the details. Huntziger and his colleagues (right) listen while Keitel reads out the clauses of the armistice conditions.*

"Should a Franco-German armistice be concluded it cannot be put into force until a Franco-Italian armistice has been signed, giving us the chance of exerting pressure.

"In the event of the Italian terms proving unacceptable, I propose to commit the fleet to a short-range action against military targets and weak sectors along the Italian coastline: 3rd Squadron [Duplat, at Toulon] – the Gulf of Genoa as far as Livorno and Elba; Striking Force [Gensoul, at Oran and Algiers] – Naples, Gaeta; and Sicily and Sardinia . . . for all available vessels under the orders of the Admiral, South [Esteva, commanding the navy in the western Mediterranean]."

If this course of action proved necessary, Darlan proposed to assume the personal sea-going command of the forces engaged in this extremely hazardous operation.

Italian indecision

But Darlan's fears as to the attitude of the Italians were proved groundless as soon as the two sides met. Mussolini was not present, and Ciano, Marshal Badoglio, General Roatta, and Admiral Cavagnari took a conciliatory line.

The Duce, probably because of Hitler's intervention, was now making very different claims to those which he had put forward at Munich. He was now limiting his extent of occupation of French territory to the zone which his armies would have conquered in all theatres of operations by the time of the cease-fire. France would be required to demilitarise a further 30-mile zone beyond this limit for the duration of the armistice. Varying levels of demilitarisation would be imposed along the Tunisian and Algerian frontiers with Libya, as well as in Somaliland.

The naval bases at Toulon, Ajaccio, Bizerta, and Mers el Kébir were also to be demilitarised. As far as the French fleet was concerned, Article 12 of the Italian list of terms echoed the requirements made by the Germans at Rethondes; but Marshal Badoglio showed himself to be much more conciliatory than his German colleague about the question of the home ports of the fleet. Moreover, he refrained from making any claims at all on French aircraft. He even went so far as to suppress the article which would have required the French Government to hand over all Italian political exiles to the Fascist authorities. On this point, therefore, Huntziger was more satisfied with the discussions at the Villa Incisa than he had been at Rethondes, faced with the brutal intransigence of Keitel.

By the late afternoon of June 24 agreement had, in principle, been reached by the two sides. But then Mussolini called Badoglio by telephone, and what he had to say should have returned the discussion to its starting-point: Mussolini wished the French to be required to give up to the Italian Army a zone of occupation which would link them up with the Germans at Bellegarde on the Rhône. In so doing, Mussolini was deferring to a suggestion by Hitler, who, forgetting his advice for moderation, had returned to the idea of establishing an Axis barrier between Switzerland and unoccupied France.

Badoglio, however, replied that it was too late and that the discussions were over; and with yet another typical piece of vacillation Mussolini yielded to his subordinate with no further argument. At 1935 hours the Franco-Italian armistice was signed, with the suspension of hostilities between France, Italy, and Germany set for 0035 hours on Tuesday, June 25.

▽ *June 22, 1940: Huntziger puts his signature to the Franco-German armistice agreement. "I hear General Huntziger's voice," wrote William Shirer, "strained, quivering. I note down his exact words in French. They come out slowly, with great effort, one at a time. He says: 'I declare that the French Government has ordered me to sign these terms of armistice. I desire to read a personal declaration. Forced by the fate of arms to cease the struggle in which we were engaged on the side of the Allies, France sees imposed on her very hard conditions. France has the right to expect in the future negotiations that Germany show a spirit which will permit the two great neighbouring countries to live and work peacefully.'"*

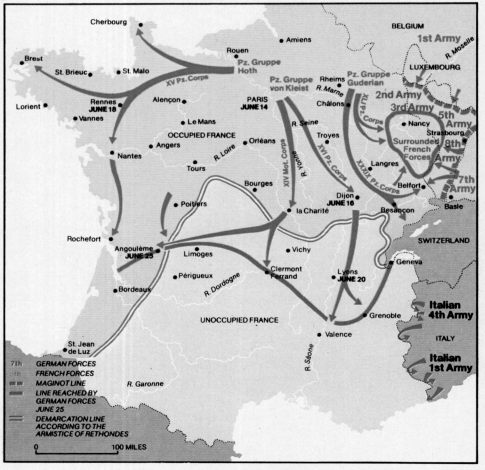

Map legend:
- Cherbourg
- Brest
- St. Brieuc
- St. Malo
- Lorient
- Rennes **JUNE 18**
- Vannes
- Alençon
- Le Mans
- Nantes
- Angers
- Tours
- Bourges
- Poitiers
- Rochefort
- Angoulême **JUNE 25**
- Limoges
- Périgueux
- Bordeaux
- St. Jean de Luz
- Rouen
- Amiens
- Pz. Gruppe Hoth
- XV Pz. Corps
- PARIS **JUNE 14**
- Pz. Gruppe von Kleist
- OCCUPIED FRANCE
- Orléans
- R. Loire
- R. Seine
- XIV Mot. Corps
- R. Yonne
- la Charité
- Dijon **JUNE 16**
- Vichy
- Clermont Ferrand
- Lyons **JUNE 20**
- R. Dordogne
- UNOCCUPIED FRANCE
- Valence
- R. Saône
- R. Garonne
- BELGIUM
- 1st Army
- R. Moselle
- LUXEMBOURG
- Rheims
- R. Marne
- Pz. Gruppe Guderian
- Châlons
- 2nd Army
- 3rd Army
- XLI Pz. Corps
- Nancy
- 5th Army
- Strasbourg
- Troyes
- Surrounded French Forces
- 8th Army
- Langres
- XXXIX Pz. Corps
- Belfort
- 7th Army
- Besançon
- Basle
- SWITZERLAND
- Geneva
- Grenoble
- Italian 4th Army
- ITALY
- Italian 1st Army
- XVI Pz. Corps

7th **GERMAN FORCES**
5th **FRENCH FORCES**
MAGINOT LINE
LINE REACHED BY GERMAN FORCES JUNE 25
DEMARCATION LINE ACCORDING TO THE ARMISTICE OF RETHONDES

0   100 MILES

The Panzers at high tide

We left the French 2nd Army Group cut off
from its commander, General Prételat, and
in great danger of being surrounded while
carrying out the retreat which Prételat
had ordered on June 14. On the 19th this
finally happened. The 1st Panzer Division,
advancing from Belfort, met the advance
guards of the German 7th Army, rushed
from Mulhouse by forced marches, at
Montreux-le-Vieux. Trapped in the Vosges
by this link-up were some 400,000 French
troops of 8th, 5th, 3rd, and 2nd Armies.

During their meeting at Munich, Hitler
told Mussolini that this last phase of the
campaign would see some bloody fighting,
but French ammunition stocks were
dwindling rapidly and General Condé,
who had taken command in the pocket,
was forces to surrender on the evening of
June 22.

When he heard of this decision, General
Duch, commanding the Polish 1st Division,
ordered his men to disperse and make for
Britain, individually or in small groups.
Many got through, while others went
underground and formed useful Intelli

gence centres behind the German lines.

During its drive on Montbéliard and Belfort, XXXIX Panzer Corps made an improvised attack on the French XLV Corps, which had been ordered to clear a passage through to Besançon. On the 17th, the 67th Division of XLV Corps–a Category "B" reserve division–had been scattered near Baumes-les-Dames. This left the Polish 2nd Division (General Prugar-Kettling) and the 2nd Brigade of Spahis (Colonel de Torcy) cut off in the bend of the Doubs river. After a fierce and gallant stand on the Plateau de Maîche, these troops were forced to cross the frontier and seek internment in Switzerland. General Daille, commanding the corps, was among the last to leave the soil of France.

The XVI Panzer Corps did not halt at Dijon, but drove onwards down the Saône valley. This threatened the rear of the French Army of the Alps, which was preparing to meet an Italian attack in greatly superior numbers between Menton and Mont Blanc. The French commander, General Olry, ordered the bridges at Lyons to be destroyed – but he was reckoning without Edouard Herriot. On June 16, in his capacity as President of the Chamber, Herriot had told Pétain that France would be disgraced by a separate peace; a few hours later, in his other capacity as Mayor of Lyons, he was ordering the removal of the demolition-charges which the French sappers had prepared at Lyons.

"*Gruppe* List", which had recently been formed by O.K.H. to reinforce XVI Panzer Corps, had taken Chambéry and Grenoble and crossed the Saône and Rhône bridges without difficulty. The French Army of the Alps would have been stabbed in the back but for the coolness and skill of General Olry. He swiftly improvised the "Cartier Detachment": 13 battalions, with 20 47-mm and 65-mm guns brought from the Toulon arsenal and which were found extremely useful in the anti-tank rôle. Olry emptied the supply dumps in the Arc, Isère, and Romanche valleys, while Cartier tackled the Germans with all the efficiency of a skilled tactician and a resolute commander. By dawn on the 25th Hoeppner's Panzers had been held on the Aix-les-Bains–Voiron–Romans line; on the right bank of the Rhône, they had taken Annonay and had reached St. Etienne.

In the centre of the German front, the 2nd Army had crossed the Loire at Nevers and la Charité; In the latter town a patrol from 9th Panzer Division discovered the entire archives of the French High Command on a train abandoned in the station. This gave Hitler information about the military discussions with Turkey, Greece, and Yugoslavia held by Weygand when he was commanding in the Middle East. According to General Liss, head of "Section West" of the *Abwehr*, these archives also revealed "an interesting military convention with a neutral Power", which can be identified as Switzerland from a note in Halder's diary dated July 21.

Between Gien and Saumur the wreckage of the French 3rd Army Group tried desperately to hold the Germans along the Loire, in the face of heavy tactical bombing attacks. At Saumur, 2,300 cadets of the Cavalry School under Colonel Michon held off the German 1st Cavalry Division for 48 hours. But on the 19th the Germans crossed the river and by the 23rd General Besson's three armies had been reduced to a strength of no more than 65,000 men still under arms.

In the west the Panzer onrush was so swift that the hope of organising a "Breton Redoubt" for French troops saved at Dunkirk and a new B.E.F. under General Brooke was soon dispelled. From his first contact with French Supreme Headquarters, Brooke had been convinced that if Britain persisted she would lose three divisions with absolutely no benefit to anyone. On June 13–14, this led to acrimonious telephone conversations with General Sir John Dill, Chief of the Imperial

◁ *The armistice is signed; the French delegates depart.*
◁▽ *What the armistice meant for France: German occupation of the industrial northern regions, with the south left unoccupied under an "independent" French government.*
△ *Derisive comment on Mussolini's ignominious rôle in the defeat of France–a Bulgarian cartoon.*

▽ *A French Alpine soldier keeps watch on the Italian frontier. Thanks to the superb fighting qualities of the French Army of the Alps, Mussolini's clumsy attempt to overrun south-eastern France was a complete failure.*

The French Fleet: trump card at the Armistice

The French heavy cruiser *Algérie*

Displacement: 10,000 tons.
Armament: eight 8-inch, twelve 3.9-inch, and eight 37-mm A.A. guns, six 21.7-inch torpedo tubes, and three aircraft.
Armour: $4\frac{1}{4}$-inch belt, $1\frac{1}{8}$- to $3\frac{1}{8}$-inch deck, $2\frac{3}{4}$- to $3\frac{7}{8}$-inch turrets, and $2\frac{3}{4}$- to $3\frac{7}{8}$-inch control tower. **Speed:** 31 knots. **Radius:** 8,700 miles at 15 knots.
Length: $610\frac{3}{4}$ feet. **Beam:** $65\frac{3}{4}$ feet. **Draught:** $20\frac{1}{4}$ feet. **Complement:** 748.

The French battleship *Richelieu*

Displacement: 35,000 tons.
Armament: eight 15-inch, nine 6-inch, twelve 3.9-inch A.A., and eight 13.2-mm A.A. guns, and three aircraft.
Armour: $13\frac{5}{8}$-inch belt, 6- to $6\frac{3}{4}$-inch deck, $6\frac{3}{4}$- to $17\frac{1}{2}$-inch turrets, and 4- to $13\frac{3}{8}$-inch control tower.
Speed: 30 knots.
Radius: 5,500 miles at 18 knots.
Length: $813\frac{1}{4}$ feet.
Beam: $108\frac{1}{4}$ feet.
Draught: $31\frac{3}{4}$ feet.
Complement: 1,600.

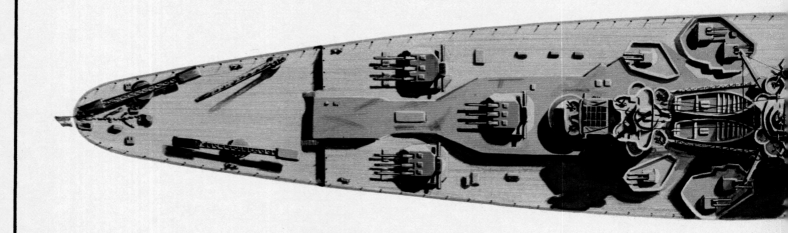

The French battle-cruiser *Dunkerque*

Displacement: 26,500 tons.
Armament: eight 13-inch, sixteen 5.1-inch, eight 37-mm A.A., and thirty-two 13.2-mm A.A. guns, and four aircraft.
Armour: $5\frac{3}{4}$- to $9\frac{3}{4}$-inch belt, 5- to $5\frac{5}{8}$-inch deck, 6- to 13-inch turrets, and $6\frac{1}{4}$- to $10\frac{1}{2}$-inch control tower.
Speed: $29\frac{1}{2}$ knots.
Radius: 7,500 miles at 15 knots.
Length: $703\frac{3}{4}$ feet.
Beam: $102\frac{1}{4}$ feet.
Draught: $31\frac{1}{2}$ feet.
Complement: 1,381.

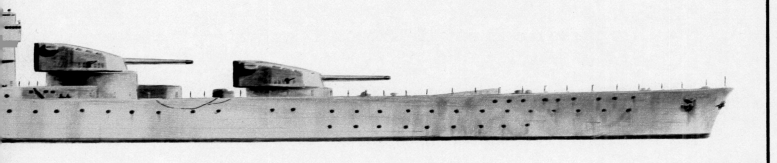

General Staff (C.I.G.S.), and with Churchill, both of whom wanted to keep British troops in action on the continent because of the alliance with France.

But Brooke's persistence in withdrawing the British forces won the day, even before Pétain had announced his determination to stop the fighting. Between June 15 and June 20 nearly 145,000 British troops succeeded in embarking; the first of them left from Cherbourg (52nd Division), the 1st Canadian Division from Brest, and the last forces from Bayonne and St. Jean-de-Luz.

It was not before time. On June 18 Rommel's 7th Panzer Division took Cherbourg; the following day 5th Panzer Division occupied Brest, and the 11th Motorised Brigade took Nantes and St. Nazaire. In the latter port, the energy and brilliant seamanship of Captain Ronarch snatched the battleship *Jean Bart* from under the Germans' nose at the last minute, although she was still uncompleted and extremely hard to manoeuvre,

▽ *Italian troops in action during Mussolini's abortive invasion of France. For most of them the armistice came as a profound relief: it saved at least one unit from complete disaster.*

with only a few inches of water beneath her keel.

During the evacuation of the French Channel and Atlantic naval bases, all warships and supply ships incapable of putting to sea were ruthlessly scuttled. This was the fate of the destroyer *Cyclone*, five submarines and two tankers, to name only the larger craft. Two battleships (*Courbet* and *Paris*), four destroyers, six torpedo-boats, seven submarines, and 13 gunboats took refuge in British ports. The order which set this evacuation in motion was cancelled after the request for an armistice was made, but the warships

leaving other ports also threatened by the Germans were ordered to make for Africa: *Richelieu* anchored at Dakar and *Jean Bart* at Casablanca. It is therefore hard to understand why Churchill wrote in *The Second World War:* "No more French warships moved beyond the reach of the swiftly approaching German power." This remark was made with regard to June 18, the day that *Jean Bart* left St. Nazaire under the bombs of the Stukas. No more French warships followed because there were no more left to do so.

From June 18 onwards the German advance in the west and south-west was a runaway victory. As had been done in the case of Lyons, the Bordeaux Government declared every town with over 20,000 inhabitants an "open town". But many smaller places, crammed with refugees, claimed similar status and hoisted the white flag behind the backs of troops who were still trying to slow the German advance. By the time of the cease-fire, XV Panzer Corps, spearhead of the 18th Army, had pushed south as far as the Marennes – Saintes – Cognac – Angoulême line.

In the north-east of France, the retreat ordered by General Prételat had left the defence of the Maginot Line to the fortress troops. Although completely surrounded and attacked from all sides, these forces continued to fight back. Around the Saar valley a small number of emplacements surrendered after their cupolas had been knocked out by direct hits from 3.7-cm anti-tank and 8.8-cm A.A. guns. But the big forts on the Lauter and between Longuyon and Faulquemont, with their guns mounted in armoured turrets, repulsed every assault despite the fire of 28-cm railway guns and 1,100-lb bombs dropped by Stukas.

On June 25, the Germans and the 220,000 Frenchmen holding the Maginot Line ceased fire; but the French garrisons did not march out until written orders reached them from Weygand. In exchange for their surrender and captivity the Germans withdrew to the demarcation-line agreed at Rethondes. So it was that St. Etienne, Clermont Ferrand, and Lyons were left free for another two years and four months.

In the midst of this disaster, without precedent in the history of France, there was a gleam of honourable success: General Olry's brilliant defence of the Alpine front.

On June 17 Mussolini, completely for-

During the last days before the cease-fire the battle for the Maginot Line went on. Although rendered completely useless by the Wehrmacht's conquest of northern and central France, the massive forts of the Line refused to surrender until ordered to do so by Weygand. Even the fire of the heavy German railway guns (above) could not knock them out. ◁ A strongpoint of the Line after the cease-fire – a rusty, battered memorial to what had once been considered "a battleship built on land" and the shield of France.

△ Italian soldiers during the last stages of the inglorious Alpine campaign. Thanks to sheer weight of numbers they managed to overrun two-thirds of Menton on the coast, but elsewhere their gains were virtually non-existent.

getting the "strict defensive" which he had prescribed for the Prince of Piedmont's army group, suddenly ordered the Prince to take the offensive without delay between Mont Blanc and the Mediterranean. In vain Badoglio argued that this ill-advised reversal of strategy was not only dishonourable but would need 25 days of preparation. He was severely rebuked by the Duce.

The Prince's forces consisted of two armies:
1. Mont Blanc–Monte Viso: 4th Army (General Alfredo Guzzoni) would attack with the *Alpini* Corps and the I and IV Corps, comprising three *Alpini* detachments and nine infantry divisions; and
2. Monte Viso–Ventimiglia: 1st Army (General Pietro Pintor) would attack with the II, III, and XV Corps, comprising 13 infantry divisions.

Behind these front-line forces of 188 infantry battalions and 2,949 guns were the eight mobile divisions of General Mario

Vercellino's "Po" Army. The task of these motorised units was to exploit the breaches made by the infantry. The five divisions of the Duke of Bergamo's 7th Army would serve as a general reserve.

Moutiers-en-Tarentaise was named as the first objective for 4th Army; Nice, and finally Marseilles, for 1st Army.

Across the Alps, General Olry found his forces reduced to the bare minimum with which to meet the Italian attack.

On the French left flank was General Beynet's XIV Corps, facing the Italian 4th Army with its 66th and 64th Divisions, (Generals Boucher and St. Vincent), and the fortified sectors in Savoy and Dauphiné (Colonel de la Baume and General Cyvoct).

On the right flank was General Montagne's XV Corps, consisting of General de St. Julien's 65th Division and General Magnien's troops in the fortified sector of the Maritime Alps.

This added up to a total of 185,000 French troops to meet the attack of 450,000 Italians. On the northern sector, between Mont Blanc and the Col de Larche, the terrain favoured the defenders. Further to the south the Franco-Italian frontier veered away from the mountain peaks in favour of the Italians, but the French had countered this disadvantage by building powerful fortifications. On the night of June 10–11 General Olry had made play with his demolitions network, and had acquired another advantage for his defending troops.

Italian failure all along the front

The Prince of Piedmont opened his offensive in bad weather, in the Maritime Alps sector, on June 20; it was to be extended to the whole front on the following day. By the time of the armistice on the 25th the Italians had managed to advance as far as the French defences in a few places; but despite Mussolini's lying and bombastic claims, Italian troops had managed to break through none of them.

At the Little St. Bernard, the *Alpini* Corps pushed down the first few bends in the road leading to Bourg-St. Maurice but could not take the ruined redoubt which formed part of the French advanced position. In the Maurienne valley the Italian I Corps, scaling the lower passes with a splendid, sporting bravado, did manage to get a few battalions into the Arc valley and to occupy the villages of Lanslebourg and Termignon. But the two French 75-mm guns in the Turra emplacement prevented the Italians from using the road from the Mont Cenis Pass; and Ciano noted in his diary that the Italians' position would have become impossible if the armistice had not intervened and allowed them to be supplied.

On the Col de Mont Genèvre, the Italian IV Corps had no better luck. After three days of effort its "Assietta" Division had taken the old Chenaillet redoubt – defended by 19 men with two machine guns. Mussolini, in a communiqué, described the place as one of the key positions in "the Maginot system of the Alps". But to reach Briançon, the fort at Janus would have to be neutralised – and the most that the artillery of the Duce could do was to slough off a few slivers of steel from the fort's cupolas. Meanwhile the French artillery scored a magnificent success: 101 shells fired by four 280-mm mortars kept ready for the task smashed six of the eight 149-mm gun turrets of the Italian fort at Chaberton, commanding the precipitous approaches to Briançon. Even so, high praise is due to the Italian gunners; knowing the weakness of their protecting armour, they stayed at their posts amid the explosions of the French shells.

In the Maritime Alps the Italian 1st Army had pushed a mile or two into the advanced positions of the French XV Corps and had overrun two-thirds of Menton, flinging whole companies against sections, and regiments against companies. But as General Montagne loyally wrote in his book on the defence of Nice, the defenders met the superior Italian numbers with well-prepared fire from 472 guns, of which half were 155-mm or heavier.

Under this tremendous deluge of fire, the "Cosseria", "Modena", and "Livorno" Divisions of XV Corps, ordered by Mussolini to "press home the attack regardless of losses", were brought to a halt by the French defence. The Italian armour never saw action. From their small defence post at Pont-St. Louis, 2nd Lieutenant Gros and his nine men kept the Corniche road blocked until the moment of the cease-fire, when a French order came through to reopen the road.

By holding off the two Italian armies and Hoeppner's XVI Panzer Corps, the French Army of the Alps fulfilled its mission brilliantly. Amid all the misery of the fall of France, Olry's army showed that its morale was unaffected. It kept south-eastern France safe from Axis occupation – and better still, it did so at an extremely low cost: 37 killed, 42 wounded, and 150 missing. According to the figures published by the historical branch of the Italian Army in 1949, the Prince of Piedmont's armies suffered considerably more: 631 killed, 2,631 wounded, and 616

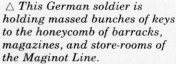

△ *This German soldier is holding massed bunches of keys to the honeycomb of barracks, magazines, and store-rooms of the Maginot Line.*
◁ *A bray of triumph in Paris: "Germany victorious on all fronts" reads this placard on the Chamber of Deputies in Paris. Notice the "V for Victory" sign, usually thought of as a prerogative of the Allies and the Resistance. The Germans were well aware of its psychological significance and were quick to turn it against their enemies.*

POPULATIONS
abandonnées,
faites confiance
AU SOLDAT ALLEMAND!

△ *German propaganda for the "New Order" in France: "Abandoned peoples, put your trust in the German soldier!" It was an obvious exploitation of the scenes of near anarchy which had been the back-drop to the French defeat—but those who believed this message would be disillusioned before long.*

missing. Most of the latter were among the dead, for when the armistice came into force all Italian prisoners were released. These totalled 3,878 officers, N.C.O.s, and other ranks. In addition there were 2,151 severe frost-bite cases.

But above all Mussolini's attack on south-eastern France threw a blinding spotlight on the weaknesses of Italy's land forces in 1940. This was not due so much to lack of courage among the troops, but to the failures of the Fascist régime which had proved itself unable to organise, equip, and lead its men properly.

All this led to considerable friction between the Italian Army and the Fascist Party.

The cost of defeat

The Battle of France was over. On the French side, the spirit of duty and sacrifice shown by some was not enough to compensate for the weaknesses of others. The French had lost 92,000 killed, about 250,000 wounded, and not less than 1,450,000 prisoners. The latter fell into two categories: those who were sent to the rear without escort after being overrun by the Panzers' lightning advances, and those who were captured because of their obedience to orders which forced them to hold their position until their means of defence were exhausted.

France suffered far more heavily than her allies in this battle. The Dutch lost 2,890 killed and 6,889 wounded; the Belgians lost 7,500 killed and 15,850 wounded; and the British lost 3,457 killed and 15,850 wounded, the latter being evacuated to England.

What were the German losses? On June 25, 1940, after the armistice, O.K.W. reckoned on a total of 27,074 killed, 111,034 wounded, and 18,384 missing—most of the "missing" being killed, as their armistices had obliged the Dutch, the Belgians, and the French to release the prisoners they had taken.

There is, however, another slant to these figures. Between May 10 and June 4 the German Army's casualty list amounted to 61,200 officers, N.C.O.s and other ranks: 2,448 men per day. With another total of some 95,300 killed, wounded, and missing between June 4 and June 25, this daily loss went up to 4,332. Effectively, it was more than doubled, since after June 18 (except in eastern France) there was no more organised resistance. If these figures are divided by the number of Allied divisions which fought in May-June 1940 we get the following result: for the first phase of the campaign—May 10 to June 3—each of the 135 Allied divisions accounted for 453 Germans killed or wounded; in the second phase, after Weygand had taken over, each French and four Allied divisions caused three times these casualties: 1,343.

Naturally, only limited deductions can be made from statistics. But in the light of these particular figures there are certain grounds for asking this question: what would have happened if the methods of command and battle tactics instituted by Weygand had been in force when the campaign began?

CHAPTER 24
Britain at bay

The defeat of France, sealed by the signing of the armistices at Rethondes and the Villa Incisa, made no difference to the determination of the British nation and its Coalition Government to pursue the war to its end. Few in Britain – with the exception of men such as the veteran statesman David Lloyd George – had thought for anything but continued resistance and final victory: they saw no reason to doubt that Nazi Germany and Fascist Italy could eventually be crushed. And the discreet attempts made by the Swedish Government to negotiate a solution to the European conflict were suppressed at birth in London.

This fierce spirit of resistance, of fight-ing back, and of final victory was incarn-ated on May 10, 1940 by the genial, picture-sque, and indomitable person of Winston Churchill. But was the Prime Minister, who was also the Minister of Defence, the universal man of war which he believed himself to be?

Churchill was indeed a man of war, if the main quality of such a man is his capacity to withstand hard blows without allowing himself to be diverted from his final objective. But if his second quality is that of concentrating his will on a principal aim and of allocating his re-sources in the correct proportions, doubts must be raised in Churchill's case. On the other hand, the remarkable adaptability

△△ *The man and the hour: Winston Churchill at his desk.*
△ *A less flattering view, this time in a cartoon intended for the conquered French. Churchill is depicted as exulting over the destruction and misery caused by his "war-mongering" policies.*

displayed by this writer-historian to all the problems of military technology must be stressed. Churchill gave his full support, among other things, to radar development and to the perfection of asdic submarine detection. Many other inventions benefited from his far-sighted imagination, despite others' bureaucratic scepticism.

Added to these talents was Churchill's remarkable skill at swaying men's opinions, which enabled him to win the hearts of the B.B.C. listening public and Members of Parliament alike. His abounding energy gave him to wide-ranging (if sometimes blundering) activity, and he possessed that hint of eccentricity which tends to appeal to the Anglo-Saxon mind. Embracing the whole were deep-rooted moral and religious convictions, extending to an unshakable belief in the providential superiority of the British nation. For the security of the latter, Churchill considered all means not only justified, but also morally desirable. Kipling summed it up: "My country, right or wrong".

To help fill out the portrait, let us look to a typical passage in the Brooke diaries, describing a conference on May 27, 1941, when Brooke was C.-in-C., Home Forces:

"P.M. in great form and on the whole a very successful meeting. It is surprising how he maintains a light-hearted exterior in spite of the vast burden he is bearing. He is quite the most wonderful man I have ever met, and is a source of never-ending interest, studying him and getting to realise that occasionally such human beings make their appearance on this earth—human beings who stand out head and shoulders above all others."

And again, on August 6, 1942, when Brooke refused to exchange his post as Chief of the Imperial General Staff for that of C.-in-C., Middle East, which Churchill was offering him:

"I could not put the real reasons to Winston . . . Whether I exercised any control or not, I knew by now the dangers to guard against. I had discovered the perils of his impetuous nature. I was now familiar with his method of suddenly arriving at some decision as it were by intuition without any kind of logical examination of the problem. I had, after many failures, discovered the best methods of approaching him. I knew that it would take at least six months for any successor, taking over from me, to become as familiar with him and his ways. During these six months anything might happen."

Germany takes the Channel Islands = the beginning of the end?

Churchill and the French fleet

But on June 31, 1940, the future Field-Marshal Lord Alanbrooke was only a corps commander in the British Home Forces. And already the brain tumour which was to kill Admiral of the Fleet Sir Dudley Pound, the First Sea Lord, was beginning to make its presence felt. The result was that Churchill's impetuosity was allowed to prevail, hurling the Royal Navy not against the Germans but against Britain's recent ally.

Hitler and Mussolini had made solemn guarantees as to the future status of the French fleet, but Churchill had every reason to believe that these guarantees were not worth the paper on which they were written. However, unless the warships were ordered to return to France, any attempt by the Germans or Italians to seize them by force seemed bound to fail – as long as they remained at their anchorages of June 25. Obviously, everything would change if the French Atlantic Squadron – composed of modern capital ships – were to return to Brest in compliance with Article 8 of the Franco-German armistice terms.

Darlan's orders concerning the action to be taken by the French warships outside occupied France were issued on June 20, 22, and 24. They were completely unequivocal; they all told the same story; and the order of June 24 is typical:

"I refer to the clauses of the armistice which have been telegraphed *en clair*. I am taking advantage of the last coded messages which I can send to make my thoughts on the subject quite clear:

1. Demobilised warships must remain French, under the French flag, with French crews, and in French ports, either at home or in the colonies;
2. Secret sabotage precautions must be taken so that if the enemy or any other power seizes a warship by force, it will be unable to use it;
3. If the armistice commission charged with interpreting the terms comes to any decision other than that expressed in (1.), the warships, without further orders, will be withdrawn from the enemy's reach – either sailed to the United States or scuttled if there is no alternative. In no case are they to be left intact for the enemy; and

4. Any warships which take refuge with foreign powers must not be used in operations against Germany or Italy without the order of the commander-in-chief."

President Roosevelt had charged Anthony Biddle, his Ambassador in Bordeaux, with taking a very firm line (not to say a threatening one) with the new French Government. The American diplomat carried out his orders on June 18 and duly reported to the White House: "[Baudouin] took pains to assure me in the name of the Government and in the most solemn manner, that the French fleet would never be handed over to the enemy . . . 'There is no question of this.' . . . Baudouin added, however, that he could not guarantee that the French fleet would join the British fleet; it could be sent to other waters, or it could be sunk."

As it is hardly likely that Roosevelt would not have passed the substance of this message to Churchill as soon as he could, the only conclusion is that the British war leaders could have been in no possible doubt that the French Government was prepared to scuttle the fleet rather than put it at the disposal of the enemies of Britain.

But the road to hell is paved with good intentions, and the British were wise to ask themselves what would happen if *Dunkerque*, *Strasbourg*, *Richelieu*, and *Jean Bart* returned to their bases in France. As we have seen, both Keitel and Badoglio showed themselves prepared to forego a literal interpretation of the armistice text: in Turin, on June 29, the Italians agreed without demur that the French fleet should be decommissioned in Toulon and in North Africa; at Wiesbaden on the following day, the Germans, though superficially more unyielding, again showed themselves to be more accommodating, for they merely forbade Vice-Admiral Gensoul's squadron to leave the Mediterranean, fearing that once it reached the Atlantic it would head for Plymouth and the British rather than Brest.

The guns of Mers el Kébir

But Churchill's decision had been made a fortnight previously. On June 17 he ordered the establishment of Force H, based on Gibraltar and centred around the battle-cruiser *Hood* and the aircraft-

Avec ce ›de Gaulle‹ là,
vous ne prendrez rien, M.Mrs..

DAKAR · MERS EL-KEBIR

carrier *Ark Royal*, with the task of watching the French fleet. A few days later he reinforced the squadron with the old battleships *Valiant* and *Resolution*, and put the whole under the command of Vice-Admiral Sir James Somerville. Also on June 17, Admiral Sir Andrew Cunningham, commanding the British Mediterranean Fleet, was told that should France conclude a separate peace, the French fleet was to be seized or sunk. The fact that the French warships which had taken refuge in England – beyond the reach of the enemy – were to suffer the same treatment, shows that the question of the French home ports played only a secondary rôle in the British plan.

Here was the origin of Mers el Kébir. When the orders came through to proceed with Operation "Catapult", Sir Dudley North, C.-in-C., North Atlantic, was

horrified and Somerville astonished. Nevertheless, they had no choice but to carry out their orders. On July 3 at 0700 hours, an officer from Force H handed Admiral Gensoul's aide-de-camp the British ultimatum. Gensoul has been criticised for not acting upon the clause in his orders which authorised him to sail his squadron to Martinique, but this is unfair. With the reduced crews manning his ships there was a real danger that they might have been stopped and captured in the attempt.

At 1656 hours on the 13th, the vessels of Force H opened fire on the four French warships in Mers el Kébir. The French ships were reluctant to return the British fire and could only clear the harbour entrance one by one. *Strasbourg* reached the open sea at 1710, but *Dunkerque*, hit by a 15-inch salvo, was forced to anchor

at the end of the bay. The elderly battle-ship *Bretagne* was hit in her after maga-zines and capsized with the loss of 977 of her crew, *Provence* ran aground, and the big destroyer *Mogador* was hit badly. Somerville ceased firing at 1732 hours and gave chase to the *Strasbourg*, but the latter escaped.

The next day, July 6, torpedo-bombers from the *Ark Royal* attacked. They did not manage to sink the *Dunkerque*, but an explosion aboard a lighter laden with depth-charges killed another 150 men of her crew. This raised the French losses over the two days to 1,297.

What were the reactions of the French Government to the British attack at Mers el Kébir? "Between 1500 and 1600 hours on July 3," wrote Weygand, "I was urgently summoned to the Hotel du Parc. I met M. Baudouin and we went to Marshal Pétain's

△ *Grim necessity to the British, brutal treachery to the French: the Royal Navy's bombardment of the French fleet in Mers el Kébir on July 3. In the background the old battleship* Bretagne, *hit in her after magazines, blows up while her sister ship* Provence, *in the foreground, prepares to hit back at the British.* Strasbourg *can be seen at the right of the picture, getting up steam for her break-out.*
◁◁ *The British bombardment was a gift for the propagandists of Germany and the Vichy collaborators. These cartoons condemn the British for their treachery at Mers el Kébir, and for their abortive attempt to take over Dakar in the name of General de Gaulle.*

△ *For vital weeks the Wehrmacht forces on the French coast had little to do but sunbathe while Hitler made up his mind to attempt an invasion of England.*
△△ *One of the heavy coastal batteries set up by the Germans to shell British shipping in the Channel—and, if the time should come, to give long-distance artillery support to their invasion fleet.*
△▷ *German troops train in an assault-boat—perfect for crossing inland rivers, but less suited to the boisterous waters of the Channel.*

office, where Admiral Darlan told us what was happening. We heard that a large British naval force was cruising off Mers el Kébir, and that Admiral Somerville had given Admiral Gensoul an ultimatum to weigh anchor and join the British fleet or to scuttle his ships. This ultimatum had been rejected and the British ships had opened fire on our warships in the Mers el Kébir anchorage, which were unable to manoeuvre or to defend themselve adequately. The French fleet replied. The unequal battle continued. We found ourselves confronted with a *fait accompli* whose consequences we could only guess at."

Weygand continued: "Much later, after my return from Germany, I discovered that at the moment when we met with Darlan the engagement had not yet begun and that the British ultimatum contained a third proposition, that of withdrawing our fleet to Martinique until hostilities ended. This proposition might have made possible an arrangement which would have avoided the need for this bloody event. But Darlan, who always kept very secretive on every question concerning the fleet—and, I think, insufficiently informed by Admiral Gensoul—served us with a *fait accompli* . . ."

At Alexandria, the good sense of Admirals Cunningham and Godfroy, and the high esteem in which they held each other, succeeded in sparing Force X, which the French had put at the disposal of the British in the eastern Mediterranean, from a similar tragedy. Cunningham, turning a deaf ear to his orders from London, did not try to force a decision by

the end of July 3; and Godfroy fought down the bitterness which the news of the bombardment at Mers el Kébir caused him. Rather like smugglers, each acting against his Government, the two admirals came to the following agreement on July 4:
1. Force X (the battleship *Lorraine*, the cruisers *Duquesne, Tourville, Suffren, Duguay Trouin* and five torpedo-boats) would be demobilised in Alexandria harbour and would land their fuel stocks, immobilising the ships; and
2. The French squadron would hand over breech-blocks from its guns and the detonators of its torpedoes to the French Consulate at Alexandria.

Drama at Dakar

At Dakar on July 8 a torpedo plane from the aircraft-carrier *Hermes* attacked the battleship *Richelieu* and put its two starboard propellers out of action. A similar operation was to have been made against the French squadron in the Antilles (the aircraft-carrier *Béarn*, and the cruisers *Jeanne d'Arc* and *Emile Bertin*) but it was called off because of American intervention.

The French warships in British ports were overwhelmed at dawn on July 3; their crews were disembarked and interned. Churchill went so far as to write, in *The Second World War*: "The whole transaction showed how easily the Germans could have taken possession of any French warships lying in ports which they controlled"—as if the question of the

French naval bases was not on the point of being settled, and as if the French sailors in Portsmouth and Plymouth would have taken the same precautions against the British as they would have done against the Germans.

Churchill's motives

To put it bluntly, Churchill wanted to strike a mighty blow at low cost to galvanise British national–and international opinion. As he wrote in *The Second World War:* "Here was this Britain which so many had counted down and out, which strangers had supposed to be quivering on the brink of surrender to the mighty power arrayed against her, striking ruthlessly at her dearest friends of yesterday and securing for a while to herself the undisputed command of the sea. It was made plain that the British War Cabinet feared nothing and would stop at nothing. This was true."

We have no way of knowing if, when Churchill wrote this after the war, he had consulted Ciano's diary. On July 4 Ciano had noted: "For the moment it proves that the fighting spirit of His Britannic Majesty's fleet is quite alive, and still has the aggressive ruthlessness of the captains and pirates of the seventeenth century."

But Ciano did not write what would have happened if the British had attacked Taranto and the Italian warships anchored there . . .

Certainly Operation "Catapult" bore bitter fruit. It caused deep and long-standing resentment in the French Navy, which, no less than its commander-in-chief, had always been sympathetic towards Britain, its former ally. The fear of a repeated British attempt of the same kind caused the French fleet to withdraw to Toulon, where it scuttled itself on November 27, 1942, in obedience to the order of June 24, 1940. The latter had not been circulated at the time of Operation "Catapult".

General de Gaulle was also profoundly affected by the drama of Mers el Kébir. "In spite of the pain and anger into which I and my companions were plunged by the tragedy of Mers el Kébir, by the behaviour of the British and by the way they gloried in it, I considered that the saving of France ranked above everything, even above the fate of her ships, and that our duty was still to go on with the fight.

"I expressed myself frankly about this on July 8th, in a broadcast. The British Government, on the advice of its Minister of Information, Mr. Duff Cooper, was clever enough, and elegant enough, to let me use the B.B.C. microphone for the purpose, however disagreeable for the British the terms of my statement may have been.

"But it was a terrible blow at our hopes. It showed at once in the recruitment of volunteers. Many of those, military or civilian, who were preparing to join us, turned on their heels then. In addition, the attitude adopted towards us by the authorities in the French Empire and by the naval and military elements guarding it, changed for the most part from hesitation to opposition. Vichy, of course, did not fail to

△ *Stukas are bombed-up in northern France. Their first participation in the Battle of Britain was in air strikes against British convoys in the Channel. When they proved their fatal vulnerability to modern fighter opposition over southern England, they were hastily withdrawn from the Battle.*

▽ *German light flak emplacement on the French coast. R.A.F. Bomber Command played almost as vital a rôle in the Battle as the fighters, constantly striking at the German invasion ports.*

exploit the event to the utmost. The consequences were destined to be grave as regards the rallying of the African territories."

And in 1962, discussing the subject with Anthony Heckstall-Smith, Admiral of the Fleet Sir John H. D. Cunningham commented: "Appallingly shameful; appallingly stupid."

Command of the sea

As in the days of Philip of Spain, Louis XIV, and Napoleon, Britain's chances of resisting an invasion from the Continent depended on retaining control of the Channel and the North Sea.

For an attack on Britain in 1940, Hitler was considerably weaker than Napoleon had been in 1805. The heavy naval losses suffered in the Norwegian campaign had reduced the German fleet to the strength of one pocket-battleship, four cruisers, and a dozen destroyers. But the enormous superiority of the British Home Fleet, based on Scapa Flow, was countered by the numerical strength of the Luftwaffe, plus the danger represented by U-boats and torpedo-boats. This triple threat would have made Home Fleet operations in the Narrow Seas far too hazardous, and the Admiralty, in the light of the experience of Dunkirk, was unwilling to risk the fleet further south than the Wash.

Thus the Channel and the southern approaches to the North Sea became a sort of naval no-man's-land. In the skies above these waters victory or defeat for the Luftwaffe would decide whether or not Germany risked an invasion attempt.

Britain's weaknesses

Would a defeat for the R.A.F. have permitted the Wehrmacht to land—as envisaged by the O.K.H. Directive of July 27, 1940—on the coasts of Kent, Sussex, the Isle of Wight, and Dorset? At the time of the French armistice at Rethondes on June 22, the British Army in Britain totalled some 26 divisions, of which 12 had been formed recently and were not yet fully trained and equipped. The 13–14 divisions which had seen action in France had lost most of their artillery and anti-tank weapons, and had brought back only 25 out of their 600 tanks. Nor had the troops been assigned equal sectors of the south coast to defend. Around Brighton, Montgomery's 3rd Division had some 30 miles of coastline to watch; between western Sussex and Wales, Sir Alan Brooke's Southern Command consisted of a corps staff and a mere three divisions, of which two were Territorial.

On June 26, Brooke wrote gloomily: "The main impression I had was that the Command had a long way to go to be put on a war footing . . . The more I see of conditions at home, the more bewildered I am as to what has been going on in this country since the war started. It is now ten months, and yet the shortage of trained men and equipment is appalling . . . There are masses of men in uniform, but they are mostly untrained: why, I cannot think after ten months of war. The ghastly part of it is that I feel certain that we can only have a few more weeks before the *boche* attacks."

This was hardly an exaggeration. On

▽ *General Sir Alan Brooke, the man responsible for the defence of Britain's southern shores, on one of his countless tours of inspection. He had no illusions about the weaknesses in the defences: "A responsibility such as that of the defence of this country under existing conditions is one that weighs on one like a ton of bricks," he wrote.*

July 19 General Ironside, C.-in-C., Home Forces, had been relieved of his post. Although he was promoted to field-marshal and given a seat in the House of Lords, this was still seen as a disgrace, since it was only two months since he had been replaced as Chief of the Imperial General Staff by General Sir John Dill. But was Ironside alone responsible for the weaknesses of the British Army? In his memoirs, Eden says not. He refers to the "surprising bitterness" with which Dill criticised Hore-Belisha, former Secretary of State for War. "He had done damage to the army that could not be repaired in years, Dill said, commanders had come to look over their shoulders."

Passing Southern Command to General Auchinleck, who had done so well at Narvik, Brooke took over from Ironside and threw himself into intense and timely activity as commander of the Home Forces. Making lavish use of aircraft transport, he was everywhere, countermanding the strict defensive prescribed to all sectors and releasing mobile reserves for counter-attacks. But this was not enough: he also had to order that the areas in which such counter-attacks might have to be made were cleared for action, by demolishing the concrete obstacles which had studded village streets since May.

Brooke's responsibilities were far greater than the resources at his disposal. In the diary which he kept for his wife, he occasionally gave vent to the anguish which the immediate future caused him. On September 15 he wrote:

"Still no move on the part of the Germans. Everything remains keyed up for an early invasion, and the air war goes on unabated. This coming week must remain a critical one, and it is hard to see how Hitler can retrace his steps and stop the invasion. The suspense of waiting is very trying, especially when one is familiar with the weaknesses of one's defences. Our exposed coast line is just twice the length of the front that we and the French were holding in France with about eighty divisions and the Maginot Line. Here we have twenty-two divisions of which only about half can be looked upon as in any way fit for any form of mobile operations. Thank God the spirit is now good and the defeatist opinions expressed after Dunkirk are no longer prevalent. But I wish I could have six months more to finish equipping and training the forces under my command. A responsibility such as that of the defence of this country under existing conditions is one that weighs on one like a ton of bricks, and it is hard at times to retain the hopeful and confident exterior which is so essential to retain the confidence of those under one and to guard against their having any doubts as regards final success."

The organisation responsible for the defence of the island was not likely to soothe Brooke's worries. If the Germans had tried an invasion they would have encountered no inter-service high command capable of co-ordinating the efforts of the British Army, Navy, and Air Force. The First Sea Lord had no less than six "commanders-in-chief" under his orders, while the Chief of the Air Staff had three. And Brooke had no authority to give orders to any of them.

"This system," he wrote after the war, "presented grave dangers. If a landing had taken place I fear that Churchill, as Minister of Defence, would have tried to co-ordinate the activity of the different commands himself. This would have been a perilous mistake, for with his impulsive nature he would have tended to take decisions according to his intuition and not from a logical perspective."

It was no less urgent to replace the *matériel* lost at Dunkirk as soon as possible, to raise the divisions still training to battle-worthiness, and to arm the Home Guard, which in August 1940 contained one million volunteers. To this end, guns were taken from military museums and

△ *The Luftwaffe strikes against the British shipping in the Channel: a near-miss on a freighter.* ▽ *No mistake this time —the death of a merchantman.*

war memorials; the Drury Lane Theatre contributed a dozen rusty old rifles; shotguns and ammunition were commandeered; and even cutlasses from the navy of Nelson's day were distributed to the local defence volunteers.

Stepping up production

Meanwhile, the arms factories were accelerating their production all the time. On June 8 there were 72 infantry and cruiser tanks in Britain; this rose to 200 by August, and there were 438 by September 29. The production rate was expected to rise to 12–15 per week for infantry tanks and nine per week for cruiser tanks. But these tanks, although brand new, were—as Rommel was to prove in Libya—already obsolescent for modern armoured warfare.

Britain took over from France the military contracts which the latter had signed with the United States and which had not been completed by the time of the armistice. But, most important of all, Roosevelt agreed to provide Britain with 500,000 rifles and 900 75-mm guns, each supplied with 1,000 shells. By the "cash and carry" principle still in force, the British Merchant Navy was responsible for bringing these precious cargoes home, and this was done with no losses to U-boat attacks. Churchill commented that certain generals turned up their noses at these 900 guns, which dated from the end of World War I. But the British were desperately short of artillery: on June 8 there were only 420 field guns and 163 heavy guns, with 200 and 150 rounds per gun respectively. And during the second phase of the Battle of France the 75-mm gun had proved its worth as a tank-killer. On June 8 the British Home Forces had only 54 2-pounder (40-mm) guns which could be used against tanks.

By September 17 Brooke had the following resources for the defence of Great Britain and Northern Ireland: 29 divisions and eight independent brigades, six of which were armoured. These forces included two Canadian divisions, the 1st and 2nd, of which only the 1st Division had suffered at all (one man killed and five missing) during its recent excursion to France. This little army, faced with invasion, was outnumbered by an estimated four to one—and on top of that it was still not ideally deployed.

Raeder prepares . . .

During the winter of 1939–40, not wishing to be caught unprepared by a sudden demand from Hitler, Grand-Admiral Raeder had ordered his staff to make a study of the many problems which would have to be settled if he were ordered to transport the German Army across the Channel.

On May 21, 1940, at the moment when the Panzers were driving onwards from Abbeville towards Boulogne and Calais, Raeder told Hitler of the conclusions reached by these studies. But the information fell upon preoccupied ears. As late as June 20 Raeder had still received no reaction from Hitler on the subject: when he made his report and asked for instructions, all he got from the Führer were some vague suggestions for a scheme to transport Jews to Madagascar.

. . . and Hitler dallies

Hitler's indifference to Raeder's invasion suggestions on May 21 was not surprising: his attention was focussed on the battle in hand. He was apprehensive that the temerity of his generals would allow the French to stage a new "Miracle of the Marne", recovering as they had done in 1914. Later, on the eve of the arrival of the French armistice delegates at Rethondes, Hitler's dilatory attitude towards Raeder was the result of his uncertainty about the best road to take now that France had been crushed. At Munich on the 18th, Ciano

had seen Hitler as an actor preparing to play the part of Charlemagne, "the gambler who has made a big scoop and would like to get up from the table risking nothing more", and wondering if there were any real advantage in overthrowing the awesome mass of the British Empire. Would Churchill see sense? Would he fall? Either of the two would make an invasion of England unnecessary.

From June 25 to July 5 Hitler remained with a small group of consultants aboard his special train *Tannenberg* at Kniebis, near Freudenstadt in the Black Forest, waiting for the situation to become clarified one way or the other. On July 2 a landing in England was certainly the object of an order—but it was only a hypothetical case, together with several others, and no preparations were to be made yet.

It was on July 16, in Berlin, that Hitler signed his famous Directive No. 16—*Seelöwe* (Operation "Sea Lion"). But the preamble to this document shows that even at this date the invasion was not regarded as inevitable. It stated: "Since England, in spite of her apparently hopeless military situation, shows no sign of coming to terms, I have decided to prepare a landing operation against England, and if necessary to carry it out.

"The aim of this operation is to eliminate the British homeland as a base for the further prosecution of the war against Germany, and, if necessary, to occupy it completely."

This was not, therefore, Hitler's final word. But a month had passed since the fall of Paul Reynaud's government and France's request for an armistice, and those 30 days had not been wasted by the British aircraft industry, ably stimulated by Lord Beaverbrook. Allowing for two more months of preparations and preliminary moves, an invasion would not be possible until September 16—on the eve of the period of boisterous early autumn weather which would make the Channel impassable to light landing-craft.

From the Reichstag on July 19 Hitler addressed an ultimatum, dressed up as an offer of peace, to Winston Churchill. Churchill was recommended, in all conscience, to make the British people see reason, for he, Hitler, could see no reason for the struggle to continue. He would not be responsible for any further shedding of blood. London made no reply to this insolent harangue; and Hitler was forced to go ahead with the build-up for "Sea Lion".

◁ △ British cartoonist David Low sums up the spirit of 1940: "Very well, alone!"
◁▽ Britain's last-ditch defenders–the "Local Defence Volunteers"–in training. On June 26 Churchill wrote: "I don't think much of the name 'Local Defence Volunteers' . . . I think 'Home Guard' would be better. Don't hesitate to change on account of already having made armlets, etc, if it is thought the title of Home Guard would be more compulsive." He got his way.
◁ Grand-Admiral Erich Raeder, responsible for the naval side of the German invasion, who did not hesitate to pass the responsibility for the success of the venture to Göring's Luftwaffe.

▽ A useful morale-booster in Britain was the slogan "From saucepan to Spitfire". A massive collection of aluminium kitchen utensils was set afoot–but its material returns were never more than a drop in the bucket.

The British Vickers Supermarine Spitfire IA single-seat fighter

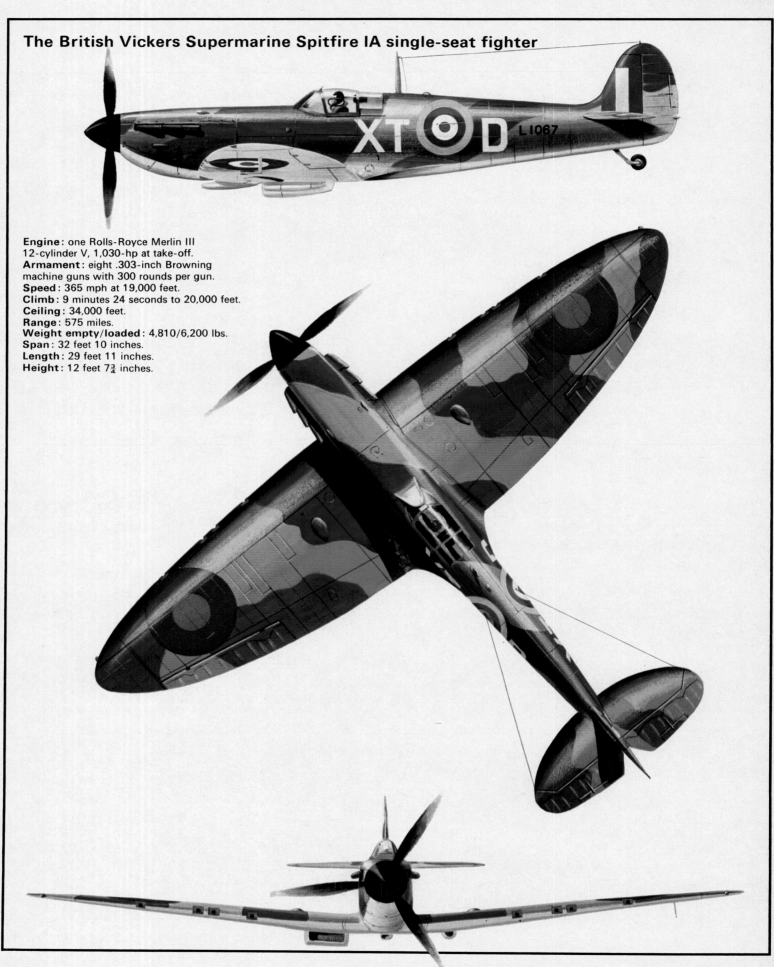

Engine: one Rolls-Royce Merlin III
12-cylinder V, 1,030-hp at take-off.
Armament: eight .303-inch Browning
machine guns with 300 rounds per gun.
Speed: 365 mph at 19,000 feet.
Climb: 9 minutes 24 seconds to 20,000 feet.
Ceiling: 34,000 feet.
Range: 575 miles.
Weight empty/loaded: 4,810/6,200 lbs.
Span: 32 feet 10 inches.
Length: 29 feet 11 inches.
Height: 12 feet 7¾ inches.

CHAPTER 25
Battle of Britain

On July 27 Brauchitsch–recently promoted to Field-Marshal, together with 12 other Army and Luftwaffe generals–submitted a preliminary invasion plan to O.K.W. With 41 divisions, six of them armoured and three motorised, plus the Luftwaffe's 7th Parachute Division and the 22nd Airborne Division, the plan read as follows:

On D-Day (set at shortly after August 25) Rundstedt's Army Group "A" would cross the Channel with two armies:

Right flank: 16th Army (Busch), concentrated between Ostend and the Somme, would land between Ramsgate and Hastings; and

Left flank: 9th Army (Strauss), concentrated between the Somme and the Orne, would land between Brighton and Littlehampton, with a detachment on the Isle of Wight.

The Gravesend–Reigate–Portsmouth line was designated as the first objective for Rundstedt's army group.

Simultaneously, or after a short delay,

depending on circumstances, Bock's Army Group "B" would launch Reichenau's 6th Army from the Cherbourg Peninsula against the Dorset coast. Landing between Weymouth and Lyme Regis it would strike towards Bristol, pushing a detachment across Devon.

At this moment the 9th Army would break the British defences along the North Downs, cross the Thames at Reading, and encircle London from the west. The second objective for Rundstedt and Bock was to be the line connecting Maldon on the North Sea with Gloucester on the Severn.

As the man responsible for the land forces during the assault crossing, and for their supply during the campaign, Raeder denounced the whole ambitious scheme as impracticable. Even by requisitioning every available vessel from the inland waterways and the fishing fleets–which would have serious results on war production and civilian food supplies–he would not be able to assure the landing

△ △ *Battle is joined: British machine gun bullets converge on a Heinkel 111 (left) and a Messerschmitt 110. Luftwaffe pilots were astonished by the manoeuvrability of the British fighters and the pulverising fire-power of their eight-gun batteries, four guns in each wing. This larger cone of fire did much to compensate for the fact that the German cannon caused more destructive hits; and, moreover, less accuracy was required than with cannon.*
△ *Direct hits on a Heinkel 111 (left) envelop the aircraft in smoke and flames; the starboard undercarriage leg has swung down. The picture at bottom right shows fragments flying from a Junkers 88, whose starboard engine has been set on fire.*

321

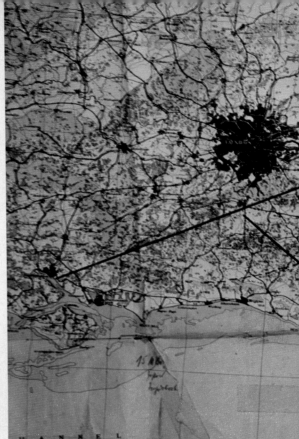

of a first wave of 13 divisions, even if their numbers were considerably reduced.

The Navy also condemned the idea of a landing on the wide front envisaged by Brauchitsch, stating that adequate protection could not be guaranteed and recommending a crossing in the Pas-de-Calais sector. But Brauchitsch and Halder in turn refused to consider feeding troops into the narrow Ramsgate-Folkestone sector suggested by Raeder and his chief-of-staff, Admiral Schniewind.

The result was a compromise. The 6th Army venture from Cherbourg was dropped completely, and O.K.H. agreed to concentrate its right flank between Ramsgate and Folkestone. But the plan for 9th Army remained unchanged, and Rundstedt would still have a sufficiently wide front for his break-out. This adjustment lowered the invasion force to 27 divisions, nine of them in the first wave, each of which would land 6,700 men on D-Day, now set for September 21. A feint landing against the Norfolk coast was also planned, to draw off the British reserves from immediately behind the landing beaches.

As there was no German battle fleet to give heavy gunfire support, and as the Luftwaffe would be unable to provide total coverage for the assault, it was decided to give the landing troops the benefit of tank fire-power. To do this, some 128 Pzkw III and IV tanks were converted to allow them to be landed offshore and descend to the sea

bed, a depth of 25–30 feet below the surface. Because of the extra 0.8 atmospheres pressure created at this depth, careful waterproofing was needed: the turret ring of each tank was sealed with an inflatable tube; and the crew and the engine got their air supply via a long, flexible snorkel tube supported on the surface, while a special valve coped with the exhaust problem. Special landing-craft with hinged ramps, and their bottoms reinforced with concrete to bear the weight of the tanks, would carry the tanks to their launch points off the British coast.

Experiments carried out by Reinhardt's XLI Panzer Corps off the island of Sylt in the North Sea proved that these submarine tanks were perfectly capable of carrying out this task. Finally, long-range artillery support was provided by coastal batteries which could reach the British coast between Ramsgate and Dungeness: four batteries between Sangatte and the north of Boulogne, with four 28-cm, three 30.5-cm, four 38-cm, and three 40.6-cm guns, with ranges of between 28 and 37 miles.

Onus on the Luftwaffe

Above all, the Royal Navy and the R.A.F. had to be prevented from attacking the sealanes which the 16th and 9th Armies would use. These extended eastward to Rotterdam and westward to le Havre. In view of the enfeebled state of the German Navy, this task fell squarely on the Luftwaffe. The latter would have to replace naval firepower on D-Day with massive Stuka attacks to neutralise the British coastal defences. But the whole operation depended on the preliminary removal from the board of the R.A.F. as a fighting force, and especially its fighter formations.

Hitler was well aware of this: his Directive No. 17 of August 1 ordered the intensification of naval and air operations against England, and the first paragraph read:

"Using all possible means, the German air forces will smash the British air forces in as brief a period of time as possible. Its attacks will be directed in the first instance against formations in flight, their ground facilities, and their supply centres, then against the British aircraft industry, including factories producing anti-aircraft guns."

When this had been done, the Luftwaffe was to turn against Britain's ports, crushing those on which the country depended for its supplies, but sparing the south coast ports which would be needed for supplying the invasion after the first landings. Finally there was to be no "terror-bombing" of open cities without the express order of the Führer: the whole weight of the Luftwaffe was to be used only on Britain's military potential.

◁◁ *The rival forces.*
1. *A Hurricane patrol in "finger-four" formation. The British soon abandoned their rigid "vic" formations of three aircraft for this more flexible "finger-four" pattern, with each leader shielded by a wing-man.*
2. *Air-to-air view of a Dornier bomber formation.*
3. *A Staffel (squadron) of Heinkel 111's in flight.*
4. *Men of the British Observer Corps sent in vital reports of the German bomber formations.*
5. *A Schwarm (unit of four) of Messerschmitt 109 fighters flies low over St. Margaret's Bay on the Channel Coast.*
△ *How the Germans planned to invade Britain. This O.K.W. map illustrates the rôle of 16th Army, which was to land in the sector between Hastings and Folkestone.*

Hermann Göring, as C.-in-C. of the Luftwaffe, made two fatal errors during the Battle. He called off the attacks on the British radar stations when they were on the verge of success, and ordered the fighters to stay with the slow, ungainly bomber streams in a defensive rôle, where they were helpless against British fighters.

Field-Marshal Hugo Sperrle was commander of *Luftflotte* III, which officially "opened" the Battle with heavy raids on August 13—*Adlertag* or "Eagle Day". Sperrle and Kesselring, commander of *Luftflotte* II, were the two principal German operational commanders in France and the Low Countries during the Battle of Britain.

Lieutenant-Colonel Werner Mölders was the greatest German ace and fighter tactician of the early years of World War II. He was the first fighter pilot to score over 100 "kills", and the first Luftwaffe pilot to be decorated with the Knight's Cross with Oak Leaves, Swords, and Diamonds—Germany's highest award.

Major Adolf Galland, like Mölders, was a veteran of the "Condor Legion" in the Spanish Civil War. After the Battle of Britain he stepped into Mölders's shoes as Germany's leading fighter ace, replacing Mölders as General of Fighters when the latter died in a crash in November 1941, and scored a total of 104 victories.

▽ *Britain's "eyes" during the Battle were the "Chain Home" radar stations which could detect the build-up of the big German bomber formations over France. This enabled Fighter Command to have squadrons brought to the alert and directed to their targets when the bombers crossed the English coast.*

The point of balance

Was the Battle of Britain lost before it began? Or did Hitler and Göring fail to make a thorough and methodical use of their advantages?

On August 13, 1940–*Adlertag*, the "Day of the Eagle"–the losses of the Battle of France had not yet been recouped by the Luftwaffe. (The French Air Force alone had caused the loss of 778 German aircraft.) To tackle England, the Luftwaffe was deployed in three air fleets:

Norway and Denmark: *Luftflotte* V (Stumpff);
Belgium and Holland: *Luftflotte* II (Kesselring); and
Northern France: *Luftflotte* III (Sperrle). On August 13 the Luftwaffe deployed 2,422 aircraft against Britain: 969 level bombers, 336 Stuka dive-bombers, 869 Bf 109 single-engined fighters and 268 twin-engined Bf 110 "destroyer" fighters.

The British, however, had come a long way since the days of the "Phoney War". Fighter production–157 in January 1940, 325 in May, 446 in June, and 496 in July–was no longer a serious worry. The supply of trained pilots was far more serious. On July 13 Fighter Command, led by Air Chief-Marshal Sir Hugh Dowding, had only 1,341 trained pilots; it would have to draw heavily upon the pilots of Coastal Command and the Fleet Air Arm, as well as forming four Polish and one Czech squadron in a few weeks.

This meant, on the surface, that this decisive battle would pit 1,137 German fighters against 620 R.A.F. Hurricanes and Spitfires–but the comparison is not as simple as that. The Messerschmitt Bf 110 twin-engined "destroyer" fighter– "Göring's folly"–was too slow and too sluggish to hold its own against the British fighters. On the other hand the Messerschmitt Bf 109E single-seat fighter was

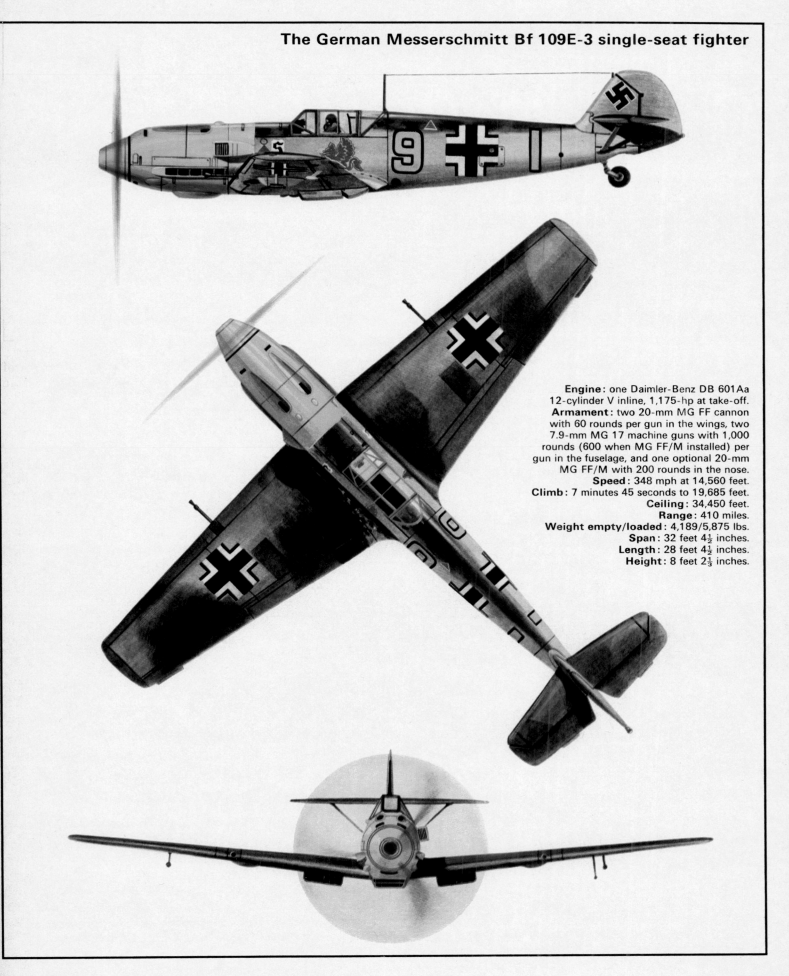

The German Messerschmitt Bf 109E-3 single-seat fighter

Engine: one Daimler-Benz DB 601Aa 12-cylinder V inline, 1,175-hp at take-off.
Armament: two 20-mm MG FF cannon with 60 rounds per gun in the wings, two 7.9-mm MG 17 machine guns with 1,000 rounds (600 when MG FF/M installed) per gun in the fuselage, and one optional 20-mm MG FF/M with 200 rounds in the nose.
Speed: 348 mph at 14,560 feet.
Climb: 7 minutes 45 seconds to 19,685 feet.
Ceiling: 34,450 feet.
Range: 410 miles.
Weight empty/loaded: 4,189/5,875 lbs.
Span: 32 feet 4½ inches.
Length: 28 feet 4½ inches.
Height: 8 feet 2⅓ inches.

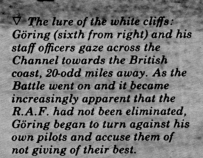

▽ *The lure of the white cliffs: Göring (sixth from right) and his staff officers gaze across the Channel towards the British coast, 20-odd miles away. As the Battle went on and it became increasingly apparent that the R.A.F. had not been eliminated, Göring began to turn against his own pilots and accuse them of not giving of their best.*

faster than the Hawker Hurricane Mk. I and about as fast as the Supermarine Spitfire Mks. I and II, although the latter machine had only begun to appear with the front-line squadrons of R.A.F. Fighter Command. The Bf 109 could climb faster than the British fighters; the British fighters were more manoeuvrable, and their batteries of eight machine guns gave them a bigger, though lighter, cone of fire than the German fighters.

Two paramount elements favoured the R.A.F. First was the defence radar network extending from the Shetland Islands to Land's End at the western extremity of Cornwall. Radar information enabled the British commanders to get their fighters off in sufficient time to avoid attack on the

ground and then, directed over the radio, to intercept the enemy, often surprising him.

Second came the fact that Fighter Command was operating largely over British soil and could recover most of its shot-down pilots. German aircraft shot down over Britain almost always meant the loss of their crews as well as their machines. On

August 15, for example, the R.A.F. destroyed 70 German fighters and bombers. Some 28 Spitfires and Hurricanes were shot down that day–but half their pilots eventually rejoined their squadrons.

For some 25 years the accepted idea has been that the German air offensive reached its peak on Sunday, September 15; during a series of German attacks on London, the

The British Hawker Hurricane I single-seat fighter

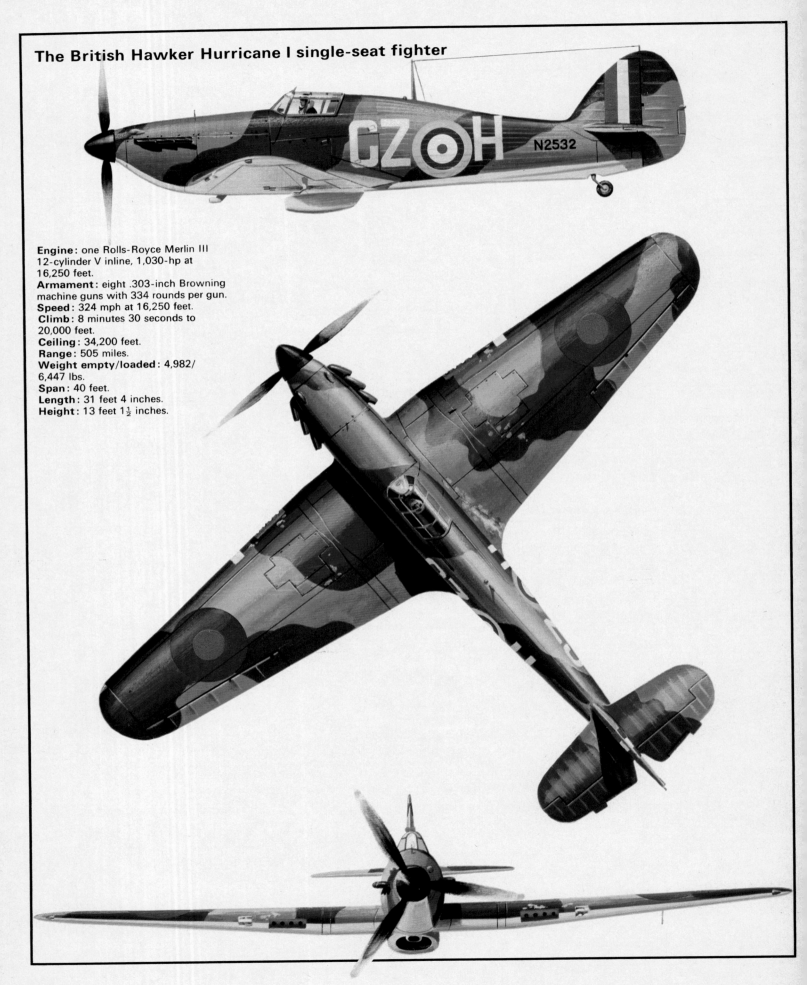

Engine: one Rolls-Royce Merlin III 12-cylinder V inline, 1,030-hp at 16,250 feet.
Armament: eight .303-inch Browning machine guns with 334 rounds per gun.
Speed: 324 mph at 16,250 feet.
Climb: 8 minutes 30 seconds to 20,000 feet.
Ceiling: 34,200 feet.
Range: 505 miles.
Weight empty/loaded: 4,982/6,447 lbs.
Span: 40 feet.
Length: 31 feet 4 inches.
Height: 13 feet 1½ inches.

Air Vice-Marshal Keith Park, commander of No. 11 Group, R.A.F. Fighter Command, responsible for the South-East. This group, under Park's brilliant leadership, bore the brunt of the fighting in the Battle. But after the Battle, Park was relegated to Training Command.

Wing-Commander Robert Stanford Tuck led No. 257 Squadron—the "Burma" Squadron— into action on September 15, the climax of the Battle. He scored two "kills" on this day, raising his personal tally to 16. He achieved a final score of 29 before being shot down in 1942.

Wing-Commander Douglas Bader, legless, opinionated, and aggressive, led the three squadrons of the "Duxford wing". His pleas for the use of fighters *en masse* caused much controversy in R.A.F. Fighter Command. Bader's final tally was 23. He was shot down in 1941 and captured.

Sergeant-Pilot "Ginger" Lacey (later commissioned) flew with 501 Squadron during the Battle. He was credited with shooting down the plane which bombed Buckingham Palace on September 13. Subsequently, Lacey served in the Far East, and finished the war with 28 confirmed victories.

British defence claimed to have shot down 185 German aircraft, a total lowered to 56 by the official post-war figures. In fact, although the British came close to defeat on the 15th they had already won, as much because of the mistakes of the German high command as the courage of the R.A.F. fighter pilots. The Luftwaffe's offensive had begun badly: in five days of operations between August 13 and August 17, the Germans lost 255 aircraft to the R.A.F.'s 184. As a result Göring withdrew *Luftflotte* V and the Stuka formations from the battle–*Luftflotte* V because it was badly placed to make worthwhile attacks on targets in northern England, and the Stukas because they were too vulnerable.

However, as long as the Luftwaffe kept up its attacks on the Fighter Command bases in southern England it was close to winning set and match. Many British aircraft were destroyed on the ground, and their essential runways riddled with bomb craters. Far more serious, however, was the fact that the operations centres, unfortunately sited on the airfields themselves and insufficiently protected against bombs, suffered heavy damage, which caused additional difficulties in co-ordinating the formations in the air.

During this phase–August 24 to September 6–the scales tilted heavily in favour of the Luftwaffe, which lost 378 aircraft as opposed to 262 British planes shot down or destroyed on the ground. On paper this suggests that the R.A.F. still had an advantage of 45 per cent–but in fact these figures were far more favourable to the Luftwaffe than might be imagined, because the German losses were shared between the fighters and the bombers. On the British side the brunt fell on Fighter Command, now reduced to under 1,000 pilots, constantly in action and desperately in need of rest.

With casualties of 15 to 20 pilots killed and wounded every day, Fighter Command was nearing its last gasp when suddenly the whole picture changed.

▽ *Hurricane patrol. As the Battle progressed the Hurricanes came to be reserved for the German bomber streams while the Spitfires tackled the Messerschmitt fighter escorts. The Hurricane was the R.A.F.'s mainstay in the Battle: there were 29 Hurricane squadrons as compared with 19 Spitfire squadrons on August 8, 1940.*

The German Dornier 17P-1 reconnaissance aircraft

Engines: two BMW 132N 9-cylinder radials, 865-hp each at take-off.
Armament: three 7.9-mm MG 15 machine guns. (The basically similar 17M bomber had a bomb load of 2,205 lbs.)
Speed: 246 mph at 13,120 feet.
Ceiling: 20,340 feet.
Range: 1,367 miles.
Weight empty/loaded: 12,400/16,887 lbs.
Span: 59 feet $0\frac{2}{3}$ inch.
Length: 52 feet $9\frac{3}{4}$ inches.
Height: 14 feet 11 inches.
Crew: three.

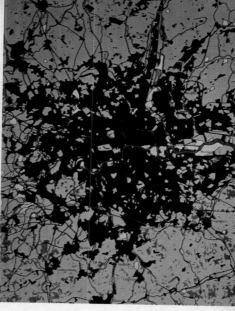

Turning-point: the London Blitz

Late in the evening of August 24, a German bomber formation accidentally bombed some non-military targets in London. Churchill's immediate response was to order a reprisal raid on Berlin. The following night, 81 twin-engined bombers took off for the German capital, but only 29 reached Berlin; the others got lost on the way. This modest raid cost the British eight men killed and 28 wounded – but this time it was Hitler's turn to lose control. Forgetting that he had formerly regarded "terror bombing" as a dangerous distraction from the main effort, he immediately ordered that London be given the same treatment as Warsaw and Rotterdam. On September 7 the first heavy "Blitz" raid broke on London, with some 330 tons of bombs being dropped.

The bombing of London continued for 57 consecutive days – but it meant that Hitler and Göring had abandoned the principal objective of the directive of August 1. The Luftwaffe was unable to smother London with terror raids without relaxing the grinding pressure which it had been inflicting on the British fighters. Fighter Command recovered rapidly: between September 7 and September 30 the British gained the upper hand over the Luftwaffe, destroying some 380 aircraft for a loss of 178 of their own.

By October 31 the Luftwaffe had lost 1,733 fighters and bombers to the R.A.F.'s 1,379 fighters – but the R.A.F. had lost only 414 pilots killed (of which 44 were Allied, mainly Poles). Churchill, therefore, was not exaggerating when he proclaimed the R.A.F.'s victory in the House of Commons

with the immortal sentence: "Never in the field of human conflict has so much been owed by so many to so few." The same praise was repeated when he wrote *The Second World War* after 1945. But at the time he was far less satisfied with the results obtained. The brilliant C.-in-C., Fighter Command, Air Chief-Marshal Sir

◁ △ *The navigator of a Heinkel searches for landmarks.*
△ *German Intelligence map of the London area, with principal military targets outlined in red.*
▽ *The Battle of Britain. Note how the British had the interior position, which gave their fighters a distinct advantage over those of their opponents.*

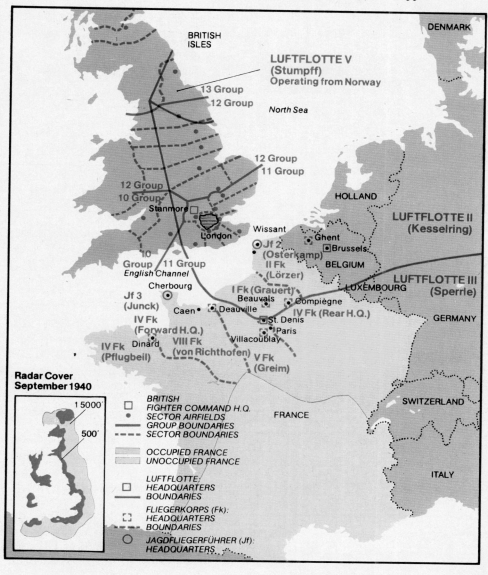

△ *The German switch of objective from the British fighter bases to mass daylight raids on London lost them the Battle.*

Air Chief-Marshal Sir Hugh Dowding has by far the strongest claim to being the victor of the Battle of Britain. Before World War II he spared no effort in building up Fighter Command into the magnificent weapon which it was in the vital summer of 1940. He stoutly resisted the demand to fling Britain's last reserve of fighter squadrons into the Battle of France, and so preserved the metropolitan fighter force which met and defeated the German attempt to gain day and night control of the air over Britain.

Hugh Dowding, and the commander of Fighter Command's No. 11 Group, Air Vice-Marshal Keith Park, the real brains behind the victory, were deprived of their commands within weeks and relegated to secondary posts. The ostensible reason was that there had been far too many faults in the field of radio communications and that the battle had been fought too much on the defensive, using "penny-packet" tactics.

The invasion postponed

Across the Channel the final preparations for Operation "Sea Lion" were being pushed ahead at an uneven pace. On shore, the troops of 16th and 9th Armies were concentrated around their embarkation points. At sea, however, the mine-laying and mine-sweeping programme intended to secure the invasion lanes from British attacks had suffered badly from attacks by Coastal Command – and Göring had failed to smash the R.A.F. Against the German invasion fleet – 2,500 transports, barges, tugs, lighters, and light craft massed in the invasion ports between Rotterdam and Le Havre – R.A.F. Bomber Command was intensifying its attacks. True, the losses of the invasion fleet were under ten per cent, but they still had to be replaced.

On September 11 Hitler announced his intention of beginning the count-down for "Sea Lion" on the 14th, which would place the landing at dawn on Tuesday, September 24. But on the 14th he decided to take three more days to decide whether or not to give the final order.

In 1940, September 27 was the last day in which the tides were favourable for such a venture. From then on into October, the high seas and strong winds which could be expected in the Channel would be too much for the inland craft to risk the crossing; they would have stood a good chance of foundering. On the 17th, Hitler ordered "Sea Lion" to be postponed. Two days later he gave the order for the invasion fleet to be dispersed in order to protect it from British bombing, but in such a way that it could be readily reassembled as soon as he needed it.

But the real implications ran far deeper. On October 12, while the ravages of the German Blitz were being extended across England, Keitel issued the following order from O.K.W.:

"The Führer has decided that until next spring the preparations for *Seelöwe* are to be continued with the sole intention of maintaining political and military pressure on Britain . . .

"Should the projected landing be resumed in spring or early summer, orders will be given for new preparations. In the meantime, it is necessary to shape conditions in the military sphere to suit a final invasion."

The German Junkers Ju 88A-1 medium/dive bomber

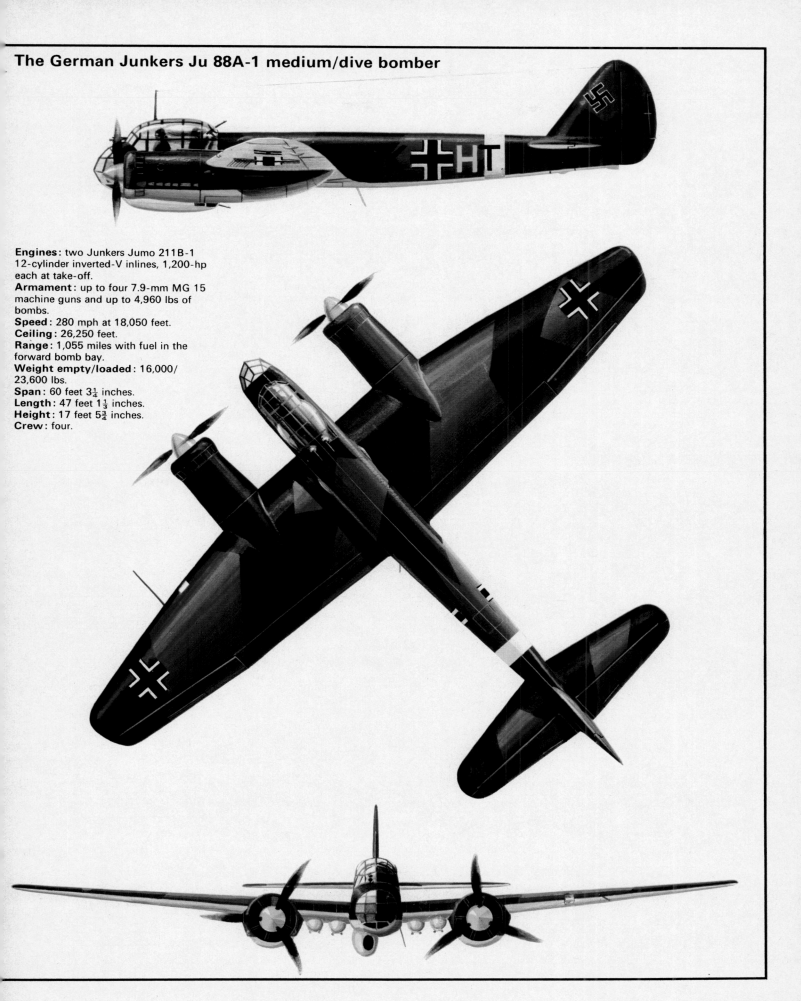

Engines: two Junkers Jumo 211B-1 12-cylinder inverted-V inlines, 1,200-hp each at take-off.
Armament: up to four 7.9-mm MG 15 machine guns and up to 4,960 lbs of bombs.
Speed: 280 mph at 18,050 feet.
Ceiling: 26,250 feet.
Range: 1,055 miles with fuel in the forward bomb bay.
Weight empty/loaded: 16,000/ 23,600 lbs.
Span: 60 feet $3\frac{1}{4}$ inches.
Length: 47 feet $1\frac{1}{3}$ inches.
Height: 17 feet $5\frac{3}{4}$ inches.
Crew: four.

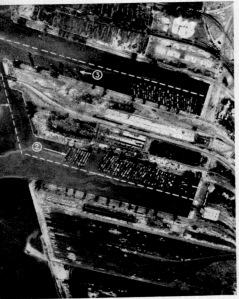

Hitler faces east

This order of October 12 reflects all the conditional uncertainty expressed in the "Sea Lion" Directive, No. 16, of July 16. Why did Hitler abandon the invasion? Was it because of the defeat which the inconstancy and presumption of Göring had brought upon the German air arm?

Certainly he had accepted that the whole idea of a landing in England had to be re-thought. On January 11, 1941, developing the subject during a visit by Ciano, Hitler compared himself with a marksman, only one cartridge in his gun, who wanted to make quite sure that he would hit the mark. But was he telling Ciano the whole truth? Or rather–having signed the "Barbarossa" Directive, No. 21, for the invasion of Soviet Russia three weeks before–was he disguising his real intentions for 1941?

To answer these questions we must examine Hitler's changing attitudes between his supervision of *Fall Gelb* in late 1939 and early 1940 and his postponement of "Sea Lion" in September 1940.

From the end of October 1939 until the end of June 1940, Hitler had been deeply involved in the planning for the invasion of France, in consultation with O.K.H. This was not all wrong: without Hitler's supervision, Manstein's suggestions would certainly have been suppressed and the outcome of the campaign would probably have been quite different. It also shows Hitler's strong desire to live up to his title of "Leader" by assuming total responsibility for the conduct of the war, and to impose his wishes on everyone.

None of this shows through between the signing of the armistice at Rethondes and the suspension of "Sea Lion". Obviously, this was a far more difficult operation for Hitler to dictate: an amphibious invasion without precedent in history. But his repeated retreats to Kniebis and Berchtesgaden, broken by a fortnight's stay in Berlin, show a certain uncertainty on Hitler's part as to the political and military decisions to be taken to assure the perpetual supremacy of the Third Reich.

No document has survived which allows us to unravel the thread of his solitary meditations. But on July 29, 1940, he spoke out.

On the afternoon of that day Jodl, head of the O.K.W. Operations Staff, returned from a visit to Hitler in the Obersalzberg.

Aboard his special train *Atlas*, which served him as a mobile command post, he summoned his deputy, Colonel Warlimont, and representatives from the three services: Lieutenant-Colonel von Lossberg, Lieutenant-Commander Junge, and Luftwaffe Major von Falkenstein. Under cover of the strictest secrecy, Jodl revealed the message which, like Moses, he had brought down from the mountain.

The Führer intended to launch an armed invasion of the Soviet Union in the following spring. As this news was received with shocked dismay by his listeners, Jodl followed with this argument:

"The elimination of the Bolshevik menace which constantly weighs on Germany renders this clash of arms inevitable. For this reason the best solution is to introduce it into the course of the present war."

Here was a singular argument, to say the least. But how had Hitler arrived at this fatal decision? Here again, documents are of little help. On June 19 at Munich, as we know from Ciano's diary, Hitler made absolutely no mention of his intention to attack Russia, although Moscow had finally put an end to the independence of Estonia, Latvia, and Lithuania a few days before.

Shortly after the armistice at Rethondes, Molotov summoned the Rumanian Ambassador to the Kremlin and gave him a 48-hour ultimatum to cede Bessarabia–a former province of Tsarist Russia–to the Soviet Union. The Rumanian Government appealed to Germany, but all it received from the Wilhelmstrasse was the advice to accede to Moscow's wishes.

The ensuing Soviet-Rumanian treaty not only restored to Soviet Russia Bessarabia–a territory which the Tsars had ruled since 1812 in defiance of the nationalist principle–but the Bukovina as well. The latter, on the north side of the Carpathians, had once been a province of the Austrian Empire, and the Kremlin had no historical claim whatsoever to it.

Was it the latter demand which precipitated Hitler's decision, being as it was a demonstration of insatiable Soviet imperialism which even a blind man could appreciate? In pushing westward the Soviet-Rumanian frontier from the Dniestr to the Prut, Soviet Russia had advanced 125 miles further to the southwest, putting its bombers within a 30-minute flight of the petroleum wells and refineries at Ploiesti–and Hitler's obsession with war economy, and liquid fuel in particular, is well known.

All the same, following former Rumanian Foreign Minister Grigore Gafencu and his captivating book *The Origins of the War in the East*, one is bound even today to return to the view that it was the failure of "Sea Lion" which provoked this total change of direction. Just as Napoleon, abandoning the idea of reducing Britain by a direct attack, recoiled eastwards and set off on the road through Ulm, Austerlitz, Tilsit, and Moscow to Waterloo, so Hitler sought in the destruction of the Soviet Union the means of compensation for his helplessness on the Straits of Dover.

It is possible that as early as the end of June 1940 Hitler had been considering the idea of an attack on Russia, but that he shelved it as his attention became more

clusively upon the short-sightedness of Hitler and Göring; for at this period their illusions were shared by every expert on strategic air power. When 36 British Wellington bombers dropped 36 tons of bombs on Turin, London announced that the Fiat factories had ceased to exist . . .

Although it was incapable of doing any serious damage to Britain's war production, the Luftwaffe's Blitz sowed fire and destruction across England and claimed over 40,000 victims, including 16,000 civilian dead. So it was that on Hitler's initiative the war was embarked on the course which between December 1940 and February 1945 would ravage Europe, from the fire raids on London to the destruction of Dresden.

◁ *R.A.F. reconnaissance pictures show the ominous massing of German invasion barges in the cross-Channel ports. Bomber Command did its utmost to sink as many as possible—but after September 19 the pictures told a very different story. Hitler's invasion fleet was being broken up and dispersed to less vulnerable target areas. The threat of immediate invasion had clearly passed.*

"HAVE I COMMAND OF DER SEA?"
"NEIN, MEIN FÜHRER."
"HAVE I COMMAND OF DER AIR?"
"NEIN, MEIN FÜHRER."
"THEN LET DER INVASION BEGIN!"

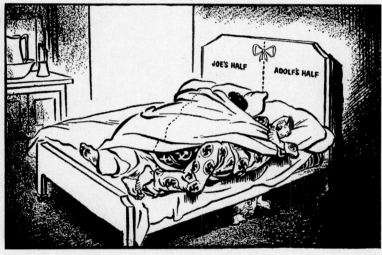

JOE'S HALF   ADOLF'S HALF

and more focussed on the technical problems of "Sea Lion". He could hardly send the Wehrmacht across the Channel to knock out Britain, the last combatant left, while husbanding all his resources for a trial of strength with Stalin.

Hence Hitler's uncertainties in the summer of 1940. With one eye on London and the other on Moscow, hoping until the beginning of September for an arrangement with the British which would free his armies for an assault on the east, he directed the battle on too loose a rein, and left far too much to Göring. The idea of adopting night bombing instead of a direct attack in order to bring Britain to her knees was totally unreal, considering the losses suffered by the Luftwaffe. Even allowing for new aircraft construction, the Luftwaffe's strength now consisted of:
898 level bombers instead of 969;
375 dive-bombers instead of 346;
730 Bf 109 fighters instead of 869; and
174 Bf 110 fighters instead of 260.

But it is unfair to dwell at length ex-

Still in the ring

By autumn 1940 all neutral powers and the occupied countries knew that the Anglo-German struggle had not ended, and that this fight to the death would not be resumed until spring. What would happen then? On July 15 Weygand had said to Colonel P. A. Bourget, who had followed him from Beirut to Bordeaux; "although British victory is still not certain, neither is that of Germany". If Weygand was talking in this fashion only 20 days after the signing of the armistice, it is easy to imagine the tremendous encouragement given three months later to the early resistance networks forming in France, Belgium, and Holland by the postponement of "Sea Lion". Now the defeat of May-June 1940 had been proved to be provisional; Hell had become Purgatory; cruel sufferings lay ahead, but they would not last for ever . . .

△ Evening Standard *cartoonist David Low ridicules Hitler's dilemma over the invasion of England (left) and over his relations with Stalin's Russia.*

EIN JAHR KRIEG

1. September 1939 bis 31. August 1940

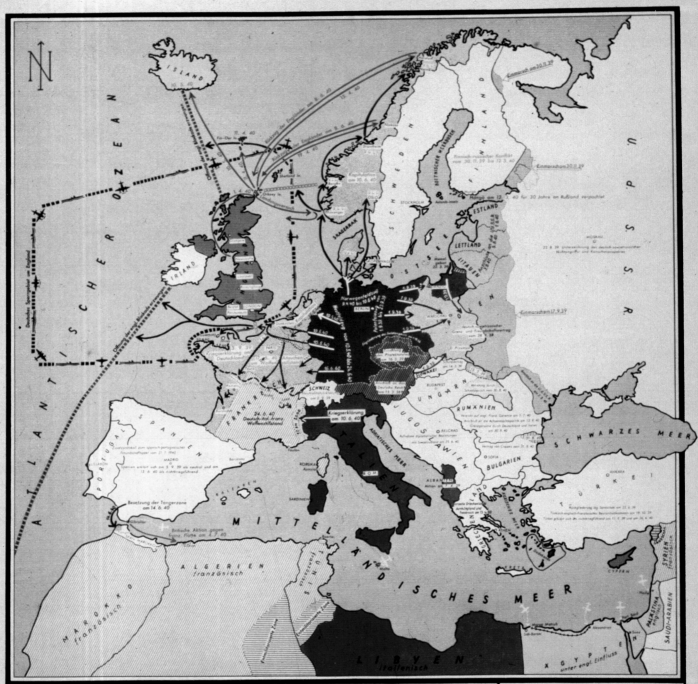

Polenfeldzug 1. bis 23. September 1939

... Polen hat den Kampf gewählt, und es hat den Kampf nun erhalten ...
Mit Mann und Roß und Wagen hat sie der Herr geschlagen.

Führerrede in Danzig

Norwegenfeldzug 9. April bis 10. Juni 1940

Dieser Schlag war das kühnste Unternehmen der deutschen Kriegsgeschichte.

Reichstagsrede des Führers vom 19. Juli 1940

Westfeldzug 10. Mai bis 24. Juni 1940

Das Gelingen dieser gewaltigsten Schlachtenfolge der Weltgeschichte ist in erster Linie dem deutschen Soldaten selbst zu danken.

Reichstagsrede des Führers vom 19. Juli 1940

Bundesgenosse Italien

Unsere Zusammenarbeit auf politischem und militärischem Gebiet ist eine vollkommene. Sie wird das Unrecht löschen, das in Jahrhunderten dem deutschen und dem italienischen Volk zugefügt worden ist. Denn: am Ende von allem steht der gemeinsame Sieg!

Reichstagsrede des Führers vom 19. Juli 1940

Führer und Feldherr

Das, was das deutsche Volk immer geahnt und gehofft hat, daß in seiner schwersten Stunde der Führer mit seinem Genie auch die militärischen Operationen lenken und leiten würde, ist zur bewunderungsvollen Gewißheit geworden.

Göring in seiner Rede vom 20. Mai 1940

Plakat Nr. 10 der RPL.

PRESSZ. ERICH ZANDER DRUCK UND VERLAGSHAUS, BERLIN SW 29

CHAPTER 26
The Duce's ambitions

Fascist Italy had entered World War II at what seemed to her leaders to be her hour of destiny. But the total and unforeseen collapse of the Allied armed forces resulted in crippling problems for Ciano and Mussolini.

What was Hitler planning next? At the time of the conference at Munich on June 19, Ciano got the impression that Hitler did not wish to risk losing his winnings. If he maintained his current attitude, would he hesitate to sacrifice the international claims of Fascist Italy on the altar of a German-British agreement, to restore the racial solidarity, so to speak, of the

Teutonic race? The Italian régime believed that a premature peace settlement would hardly suit Italy's interests, as was proved by the fact that the French-Italian armistice had yielded Mussolini nothing more than Menton and two or three Alpine villages.

But although the Fascist leaders were not eager to see a rapid end to hostilities, they certainly did not want to associate their German allies in any military ventures upon which Italy might embark in pursuit of her claims in the Balkans and the Mediterranean. This would only have meant offering Hitler a share of the

◁ *"One Year of War"–A German poster proclaims the Reich's break-out from the "encirclement" of 1939.*
△ *Italian bomber crewmen by their aircraft. Despite its convincing numerical superiority in the Mediterranean theatre the Italian Air Force soon proved its inadequacies. During the first brush between the British and Italian fleets the Italian bombers did virtually no damage to the enemy–and they launched as many attacks on their own warships as against the British.*

spoils, and as the past history of the Axis had revealed that Germany always desired at least 50 per cent of the cake it is not hard to understand the Italian doubts.

Hitler's contempt for weaker members of the Fascist Party – men like "that swine", as he called Minister of Justice Count Dino Grandi – extended to King Victor Emmanuel III and the House of Savoy, the Pope and the Vatican, and to the entire aristocracy and bourgeoisie of the country. If, as he believed, "traitors" abounded in the most secret councils of his friend Mussolini, there was all the more reason to reveal only the sketchiest hints of his projects to the Duce, and even then to do it as late as possible.

In his distrustful attitude towards Italy Hitler found no opposition from his generals. Quite the contrary: all of them had fought in World War I and remembered what they called Italy's "defection" from the alliance of the Central Powers to the Allied *Entente* in May 1915. Nor were these professional soldiers in the least impressed by Mussolini's martial swaggering. They strongly suspected that although Fascist Italy's military structure looked impressive, it was built of plaster rather than marble.

As we have seen, the Germany Army High Command had opposed the suggestion to employ an Italian army in Alsace during the last stage of the Battle of France. While armistice negotiations were still in progress, a suggestion from General Mario Roatta, Deputy Chief-of-Staff of the Italian Army, caused great indignation in his colleague Halder, who noted in his diary on June 24: "The Italians are halted before the French fortifications and are getting nowhere. But in the armistice negotiations they still want to secure an occupied zone of French territory which will be as big as they can get. To this end they have proposed sending to List's front a certain number of Italian battalions to be flown in by air, either by way of Munich or direct to Lyons, and to have them occupy the areas to which Italy wants to extend her right of occupation. All this is nothing more or less than a piece of the most vulgar deception. I have stated that I refused to be associated with the whole business."

Marshal Badoglio, however, also refused to put his name to this sordid project, drawing from Halder the complimentary statement: "According to all appearances, he is the only real soldier among this whole delegation of negotiators."

There can be no doubt that the forthright opinions expressed in Halder's diary were shared by every general close to Hitler and capable of influencing the Führer's decisions.

With all this political and psychological friction there could be no question of the two Axis partners co-ordinating their

△ *Cartoon by Lino Palacia of* La Razón *shows that the flaws in the Axis relationship were visible even in Buenos Aires.*
Hitler: *'Want a push?'*
Mussolini: *'Okay, but not too hard. I'm frightened of getting seasick . . .'*
▷ *Italian Army spit and polish:* Bersaglieri *parade with 47-mm anti-tank guns – an arm in which most Italian units were pitifully weak. Reforms in basic equipment and supply were long overdue when Mussolini went to war – and the man who suffered was the Italian soldier.*

efforts with a common objective in view, as Britain and the United States would do after Pearl Harbor. Still less was there any chance of creating an Axis counterpart to the Allied Combined Chiefs-of-Staff in Washington, where, although discussions were often acrimonious, the final decisions reached were religiously carried out.

Rome and Berlin therefore followed a system of "parallel war", but with astonishing mutual concealment and even double-dealing. Both General Efisio Marras, for all his title of "Italian Liaison General at O.K.W.", and his opposite number attached to the *Comando Supremo*, General von Rintelen, were scantily, badly, and tardily informed of the intentions of the two dictator-warlords.

The Germans were understandably incensed when, on October 28, 1940, they found that Mussolini had concealed his intention to invade Greece until the last moment. "Shocking and stupid!" exclaimed Keitel, when he heard the news of the first Italian defeats on the Albanian front. Certainly Keitel had a point, for all the harshness of its expression. But what did Keitel say when Hitler made his decision to make a total reversal of his policy and invade Soviet Russia, without informing Mussolini?

Germany's anger about Mussolini's Greek campaign is well attested. "In November I went to Innsbruck to meet the German Chief-of-Staff, Marshal Keitel," wrote Badoglio. "He immediately pointed out that we had launched an offensive against Greece without having made the least notification to the German Command. The Führer was adamant that the situation in the Balkans must not be disturbed. Germany was receiving important supplies from those countries, which she now seemed in danger of losing. 'If I had known,' said Keitel, 'I would soon have come to Rome to halt this campaign.'

"I had to tell him the truth, that I had been ordered by Mussolini to say nothing to Germany. He had in fact given me this order, and when I commented that an alliance put certain obligations on us, Mussolini replied furiously: 'Did they ask us anything before attacking Norway? Did they ask our opinion when they wanted to start the offensive in the West? They have acted precisely as if we did not exist. I'll pay them back in their own coin.'"

One would certainly have expected an operation aiming at the conquest of

Greece, and above all of the Greek archipelago, to have been on the agenda of Mediterranean strategy at the Brenner Pass conference on October 4, 1940. No operation of the scale of Operation "Barbarossa", the invasion of Russia, was mentioned – a venture which could have been only prejudicial to Italy's interests in the immediate future.

In attacking the Soviet Union, Hitler proposed to deprive Britain of the last ally which she could win on the Continent. But the relaxation of the pressure of the combined forces of the Wehrmacht on Britain could mean only that the joint enemy of the Axis would be able to recover a certain freedom of action.

Such was the system of "parallel war" which Mussolini congratulated himself upon having established against the wishes of his ally and friend. He was confirmed in his euphoria by another factor: when Churchill ignored Hitler's "peace offer" at the end of June 1940, it meant that the war would continue. And

△ *Fascist propaganda in Rome: "Mussolini is always right". Was it true that in Italy the man in the street went reluctantly to war in 1940? Sir David Hunt, then an Intelligence officer, thinks not. "I believe, on the contrary, that the war of 1940 was the most popular war the Italians were ever engaged in . . . For the first five months of the war at least, all the prisoners we and the Greeks took spoke with great confidence of a successful outcome and boasted of the future greatness of Italy, victorious at the side of Germany."*

The Italian battleship *Conte di Cavour*

Displacement: 26,140 tons.
Armament: ten 12.6-inch, twelve 4.7-inch, eight 3.9-inch A.A., eight 37-mm A.A., and twelve 20-mm A.A. guns.
Armour: 10-inch belt, $5\frac{1}{2}$-inch deck, 11-inch turrets, and $10\frac{1}{4}$-inch control tower.
Speed: 26 knots.
Length: 613 feet.
Beam: 92 feet.
Draught: 30 feet.
Complement: 1,236.

The Italian light cruiser *Giovanni delle Bande Nere*

Displacement: 5,200 tons.
Armament: eight 6-inch, six 3.9-inch A.A., eight 37-mm A.A., and eight 13.2-mm A.A. guns, plus four 21-inch torpedo tubes and two aircraft.
Armour: 1-inch sides, $\frac{3}{4}$-inch deck, 1-inch turrets, and $1\frac{1}{2}$-inch control tower.
Speed: 30 knots.
Length: 556.8 feet.
Beam: 51 feet.
Draught: 16 feet.
Complement: 521.

as Mussolini said to Badoglio on September 22: "I am happy that the war will not end quickly, for that would be to our total disadvantage. A rapid peace would be a setback for us."

Mussolini, warlord

But again the Duce was forgetting the enormous deficiencies in armaments with which Fascist Italy had gone to war, and the impossibility of making them good in a prolonged war because of Italy's lack of adequate raw materials. It was only a few months since the plain facts had been put before him and he had said to his Chief of

command. No Napoleon, in fact.

An important source is the diary of General Quirino Armellini, Badoglio's main colleague at *Comando Supremo*. Despite the fact that Armellini was opposed to the Fascist régime, the notes which he took between May 11, 1940 and January 26, 1941 – when he was disgraced – are not totally malevolent and tell an eloquent story.

The Alpine offensive had not yet begun when he wrote, on June 21: "The longer I stay at this post, the more I see of the disorder, lack of preparation, and muddle in every sphere, which seriously delays or completely prevents the functioning of the High Command; the more I believe that military necessities are being completely

▽ *Running the gauntlet to Malta: an Italian bomb bursts in the sea between two British merchantmen. In the early stages the Italian attacks were comparatively feeble and losses were slight.*

the General Staff: "This time I will declare war, but I will not wage it. This way I will get big results for using little effort."

On assuming supreme command, however, Mussolini was soon to give the most obvious proof of his lack of military talent. Before his contemporaries, Benito Mussolini, with his strutting stance, jutting chin, hand on hip or thumb hooked in belt, certainly acted the part of a dynamic and resolute commander. Even today, he is represented by the conformist and ill-informed historical viewpoint as a despot who imposed his inexorable will upon the Italian people, after deep and inhuman meditation. But eye-witness accounts and documents show his weathercock nature, his inability to make a decision and stick to it, his lack of method, his ignorance of the basic problems of organisation and

overlooked; and the more I am convinced that everything has yet to be done, or must be done again."

On August 15 he was more bitter still. "What once seemed an interesting prospect today disgusts me! We continue in the greatest disorder and complete chaos. In *Comando Supremo*, everyone commands. The last man to speak is always right. Strategic conceptions are regularly reversed with an astonishing lack of logic.

"Someone will say: 15 days from now we must be ready to march against Yugoslavia; or, in eight days we will attack Greece from Albania – as easily as saying, let's have a cup of coffee. The Duce hasn't the least idea of the differences between preparing for war on flat terrain or in mountains, in summer or in winter. Still less does he worry about the fact that

341

The British aircraft-carrier *Illustrious*

Displacement: 23,000 tons.
Armament: sixteen 4.5-inch dual purpose, forty-eight 2-pdr A.A., and eight 20-mm A.A. guns, plus 36 aircraft.
Armour: 4½-inch belt, 2½- to 3-inch deck, 4½-inch hangar sides.
Speed: 31 knots.
Length: 753½ feet.
Beam: 95¾ feet.
Draught: 24 feet.
Complement: 1,392.

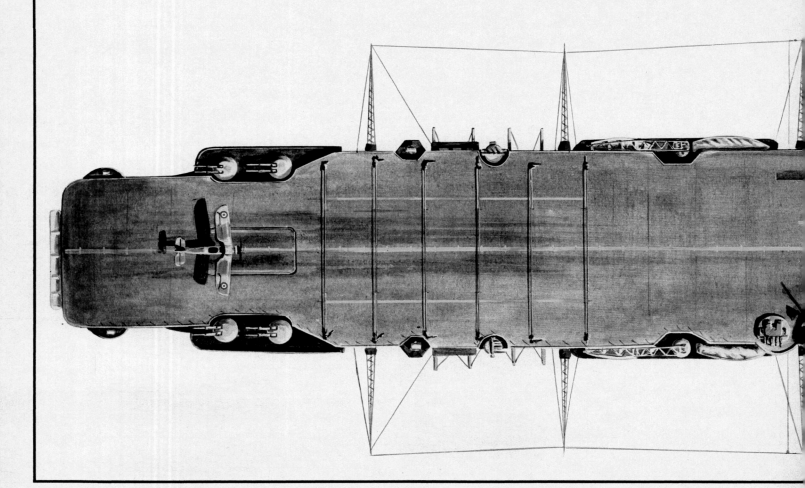

we lack weapons, ammunition, equipment, animals, raw materials."

Armellini's laments are typical of many, and all would be disastrously confirmed on the battlefield. But when blaming Mussolini and the Fascist régime, how much of the military chaos can be laid at the door of Marshal Badoglio, and, in more general terms, of the Italian Army? In 1946, Badoglio stated that his resignation "would not have resolved the situation", for Mussolini would never have

one back on his pact with Hitler; and Badoglio added: "By retaining my position, I could at least prevent some disastrous move from being made; for this was all which could have been expected from Mussolini, who was completely lacking in any military knowledge."

Badoglio had not invented this explanation to defend himself. On August 15, 1940, he had said to Armellini: "Although it may be a small thing, perhaps I can do more with him than someone else. We

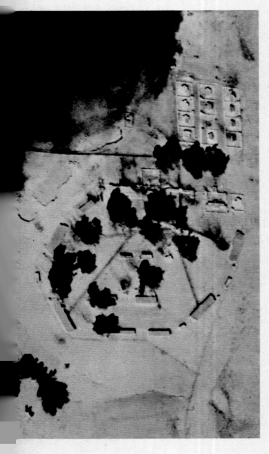

▷ *Mussolini's pride: the Italian fleet, dressed overall for a peace-time review. In the summer of 1940 the Italian fleet, with its bases dominating the central Mediterranean, was a crucial factor. Would it cause the fall of Malta by striking at the British supply convoys? And could the British, only slightly outnumbered ship for ship but forced to operate from Gibraltar and Alexandria, keep Malta's lifeline open?*
▽ *Italian bomb bursts, straddling a British camp, herald Graziani's offensive.*

must carry on, saving what can be saved, and trying to avoid sudden moves which could lead to more serious consequences."

Writing on St. Helena after Waterloo, Napoleon had thought very differently. "A commander-in-chief cannot take as an excuse for his mistakes in warfare an order given by his minister or his sovereign, when the person giving the order is absent from the field of operations and is imperfectly aware or wholly unaware of the latest state of affairs.

"It follows that any commander-in-chief who undertakes to carry out a plan which he considers defective is at fault; he must put forward his reasons, insist on the plan being changed and finally tender his resignation rather than be the instrument of his army's downfall."

No sooner, however, had Italy entered the war than setbacks assailed her in all theatres of operations.

The air and sea offensive ordered by Mussolini never got off the ground. What was worse, by June 29 the Italian Navy had lost ten out of the 117 submarines with which it had entered the war, sunk in the Red Sea and the Mediterranean. There was a very good reason for the losses (4 boats) of Italian submarine flotilla based on Massawa in the Red Sea: far too often, when submerged, the accumulator batteries of the submarines gave off poisonous fumes which rendered the crew unconscious.

In Libya, as mentioned above, Marshal Balbo had been ordered to remain on the defensive. If the reports of *Comando Supremo*'s military Intelligence can be taken as correct this was a somewhat odd decision, for 14 centrally-based Italian divisions were opposed by only eight French and five British divisions. But the situation was complicated by an exaggerated interpretation of Allied strength made by the *Servizio Informazioni Militari*. This did not dissuade Mussolini from going to war, but it did paint the strategic picture in excessively pessimistic colours.

On June 10, 1940, the French C.-in-C., North Africa, General Noguès, did have eight divisions under his command; but apart from the fact that three of them were not operational, they were deployed between the Libyan frontier and Spanish Morocco. The *Servizio* on the other hand, reported the French divisions as being massed between Bizerta and the Mareth Line, ready for an invasion of Libya.

General Sir Archibald Wavell, the British Commander-in-Chief, Middle Ea had a total strength of five divisio (about 100,000 men), but of these on 36,000 were in Egypt. They were form into two incomplete divisions: Majo General M. O'Moore Creagh's 7 Armoured Division and Major-General Neame's (from August Major-General M. Beresford-Peirse's) 4th Indian Divisic

In Libya, the Italian forces were d posed as follows:
West: 5th Army (General Italo Ga boldi), consisting of X, XX, and XX Corps, with six infantry divisions a two Black Shirt divisions;
East: 10th Army (General Frances Berti) consisting of XXI and XXII Cor with three infantry divisions, one Bla Shirt division, and one Libyan nati division.

A fourth division (the 2nd Liby. Division) was moving up from Tripoli Benghazi.

All in all, there were in Italian Nor Africa slightly over 236,000 officer N.C.O.'s and other ranks, 1,811 guns, 3 light tanks, 8,039 trucks and 151 first li aircraft. The Italian air strength was co paratively weak, but even so was stronger than that of the British.

The armistice with France was a bitt disappointment to Marshal Balbo. He h hoped that the occupation of Tunis would put the port of Bizerta at l disposal, allowing him to draw on t material and military supplies in t province. Instead of this, he had to conte himself with the demilitarisation of t Mareth Line.

The Italians were kept off balance f another reason: the British 7th Armour Division did not imitate the action of t Italian 10th Army and remain on t defensive. Instead, it launched da armoured and motorised raids across t Libyan frontier, which led the Italians believe that their weapons were inferic On June 20 Balbo wrote to Badoglio: "O light tanks, already old and armed on with machine guns, are completely ou classed. The machine guns of the Briti armoured cars pepper them with bulle which pierce their armour easily. We ha no armoured cars. Our anti-tank defenc are largely a matter of make-do; o modern weapons lack adequate ammur tion. Thus the conflict has taken on t character of steel against flesh, whi only too easily explains certain episod which are luckily of little importance."

There was nothing surprising about t

344

failure of the Italian L-3-33/5 3-ton light tank in Libya, for the "sardine-can", as Franco's men had dubbed it, had cut a sorry figure as early as the Spanish Civil War. One is, however, surprised to read that on June 25 Badoglio announced to Balbo that 70 "magnificent" M-11 tanks were on their way to Libya. In fact this 11-ton tank could be knocked out by any gun with a calibre larger than 20-mm. The standard British anti-tank gun was the 2-pounder (40-mm), and no one in Italy could have been unaware of the fact.

The threat to Egypt

On June 28, on hearing the news that French North Africa would remain loyal to the Government of Marshal Pétain, *Comando Supremo* ordered Balbo to invade Egypt with his total force, even if this meant "cannibalising" the 5th Army. But Balbo never got the order. On the same day he was shot down over Tobruk by his own gunners during the confusion of an alert.

Marshal Rodolfo Graziani, Army Chief-of-Staff, took over Balbo's command and mission, and D-Day was fixed for July 15, 1940.

In the post which he had just left, Graziani had constantly urged Balbo to take the initiative; but as soon as he arrived in Libya he too began to raise the same arguments against an advance which his predecessor had used. His task was not an easy one. There was only one supply-route across the desert between the Libyan frontier and Alexandria, on which were the British bases of Sidi Barrani and Marsa Matrûh. Graziani was not prepared to advance until he had received sufficient trucks and water tankers to supply his transport and the needs of the troops. Moreover, considering the heat of the African summer, he would have preferred to delay the conquest of Egypt until October.

But Mussolini would not hear of this. He wanted to launch the offensive on the same day as the first Germans landed in England. This led to painful scenes between Graziani and *Comando Supremo*, a visit by Graziani to Rome, and, on August 19, a peremptory telegram from Mussolini which concluded: "Marshal Graziani, as I have already told you since our last discussion, time is working against us. The loss of Egypt will be the

△ and ▽ Motorised warfare, Italian style. After weeks of wrangling and procrastination, Marshal Graziani's invasion finally got under way on September 13. On the 16th, after a 60-mile advance, the Italians reached Sidi Barrani and dug in. The trucks in the photograph below are carrying light artillery en portée. Note the immaculate tropical uniforms of the officers in the front seats.

coup de grace for Great Britain, while the conquest of that rich country, necessary for our communications with Ethiopia, will be the great reward for which Italy is waiting. That you will procure it, I am certain."

Nevertheless, 10th Army's offensive did not get under way until September 13. Four divisions and an armoured group crossed the frontier, commanded by General Annibale Bergonzoli, C.-in-C. XXIII Corps. Difficult terrain, temperatures at times over 50 degrees Centigrade, sand storms, and anti-tank mines slowed the Italian advance to a bare $12\frac{1}{2}$ miles per day. In the afternoon of September 16 the "23rd of March" Black Shirt Division occupied Sidi Barrani. This advance had cost the Italians 120 dead and 410 wounded; the British 7th Armoured Division, which had been ordered to fall back before the advance, had lost 50 men.

In taking Sidi Barrani, Graziani had covered 60 of the 315 miles between the Libyan frontier at Sollum and Alexandria, and was 75 miles from his next objective, Marsa Matrûh. But before moving on Matrûh Graziani was determined to halt

until the damage done by the retreating British had been repaired; until the *Via Balbia*, the main road which ran across Libya along the coast, had been extended to Sidi Barrani, where the road to Alexandria began; to set up a fresh-water pipeline; and to stock Sidi Barrani with provisions, ammunition, and fuel. Graziani, a veteran colonial general, was entirely correct in taking all these precautions, for Wavell was hoping to see the Italian forces over-extend themselves by a premature dash on Matrûh.

Mussolini was disappointed by the pause in the offensive. But he consoled himself by reflecting that although the Italians had not passed Sidi Barrani, the Germans had not crossed the Channel.

Hitler restrains Mussolini

Mussolini had nobody but himself to blame for the sluggishness and delays of Graziani. If Mussolini had not kept the greater part of the resources which had been released by the Franco-Italian armistice in Italy, things might have turned out very differently during the invasion of Egypt. But at the beginning of July he had decided to smash Yugoslavia, that "creation of Versailles" which had to disappear like the others.

As a result three armies, totalling some 37 divisions, were concentrated in north-eastern Italy. But Hitler was anxious that peace should not be disturbed in this corner of the Continent. On August 17 Ribbentrop, via Ambassador Dino Alfieri, informed Ciano of the Führer's opposition to any venture against Yugoslavia or Greece. Mussolini had to yield, but what was he to do with the armies which were now left without a mission? For reasons of economy, 600,000 soldiers ·were demobilised and sent home, to be remobilised a few weeks later.

In the summer of 1940, as far as circumstances permitted, the maritime honours went to the Royal Navy, which more than lived up to its aggressive tradition.

Is it fair to blame the Italian admirals for their lack of offensive spirit? They were certainly kept on a far shorter rein by the Italian High Command in Rome – *Supermarina* – than were their opponents. But one reason for *Supermarina*'s reticence was the early realisation that the Italian Air Force was not to be relied upon, whether for reconnaissance missions or for combat.

This was shown clearly during the action off Cape Spartivento on the Calabrian coast on July 9, 1940. The Italian fleet, under Admiral Campioni, was returning to base after having excorted an important convoy carrying troops and material to Benghazi. The British Mediterranean Fleet, under Admiral Cunningham, was also at sea; it was well informed about the movements of the Italian fleet, by aircraft operating from Malta and from the aircraft-carrier *Eagle*; and Cunningham planned to intercept the Italians during their return to Taranto.

Cunningham did not succeed, but the battleship *Warspite* managed to hit the Italian battleship *Giulio Cesare* at a range of 26,000 yards. Campioni broke away under the cover of a smoke screen, and Cunningham, having closed to within 25 miles of the Italian coast, also withdrew. On this occasion the Italian Air Force showed all its weaknesses; no dive-bombing or torpedo attacks were made during the encounter, and only one of the 1,000 bombs dropped scored a hit – on the cruiser *Gloucester*.

This inaccuracy did have its good side: it spared the Italian fleet from heavy losses, when Campioni's ships were enthusiastically bombed by the Savoia-Marchetti 79's of the Italian Air Force. On July 13 Ciano noted in his diary: "The real controversy in the matter of naval armament is not between us and the British, but between our Air Force and our Navy."

Nevertheless, Mussolini announced with a straight face that within three days half the British naval potential in the Mediterranean had been eliminated. On July 19 there was another encounter in the Antikithera Channel off the northwest coast of Crete. The Italian light cruisers *Bartolomeo Colleoni* and *Bande Nere*, which were heading for Leros in the Dodecanese, fell in with the Australian light cruiser *Sydney* and five destroyers. Hit in her engine-rooms, the *Colleoni* was immobilised and sunk by torpedoes, while the *Bande Nere* escaped. This was a clear indication of combat weaknesses of these light warships, in which protection had been sacrificed for the sake of speed.

In early August, however, the naval balance in the Mediterranean appeared to shift heavily in Italy's favour. The battleships *Littorio*, *Vittorio Veneto*, *Caio Duilio*, and *Andrea Doria* joined the Italian fleet. The first two were powerful,

▽ *Aboard the* Cesare *after the clash off Cape Spartivento: an Italian damage party surveys the havoc wrought by a shell from the* Warspite.

modern warships displacing over 41,000 tons, with a main armament of nine 15-inch guns and a top speed of 28 knots. The others were battleships which had been launched in 1913 and completely overhauled in the late 1930's. The two *Doria*-class battleships were each armed with ten 12.6-inch guns and could make 26 knots.

From its central position this formidable battle fleet outnumbered the combined squadrons of Admirals Somerville and Cunningham by six capital ships to five, the British squadrons being separated at opposite ends of the Mediterranean. The British still had a slight advantage in firepower, but none of the battleships in the Mediterranean Fleet was faster than 24 knots. After the affair off Calabria, the British Admiralty sent to the eastern

The British Fairey Swordfish Mark I torpedo-bomber

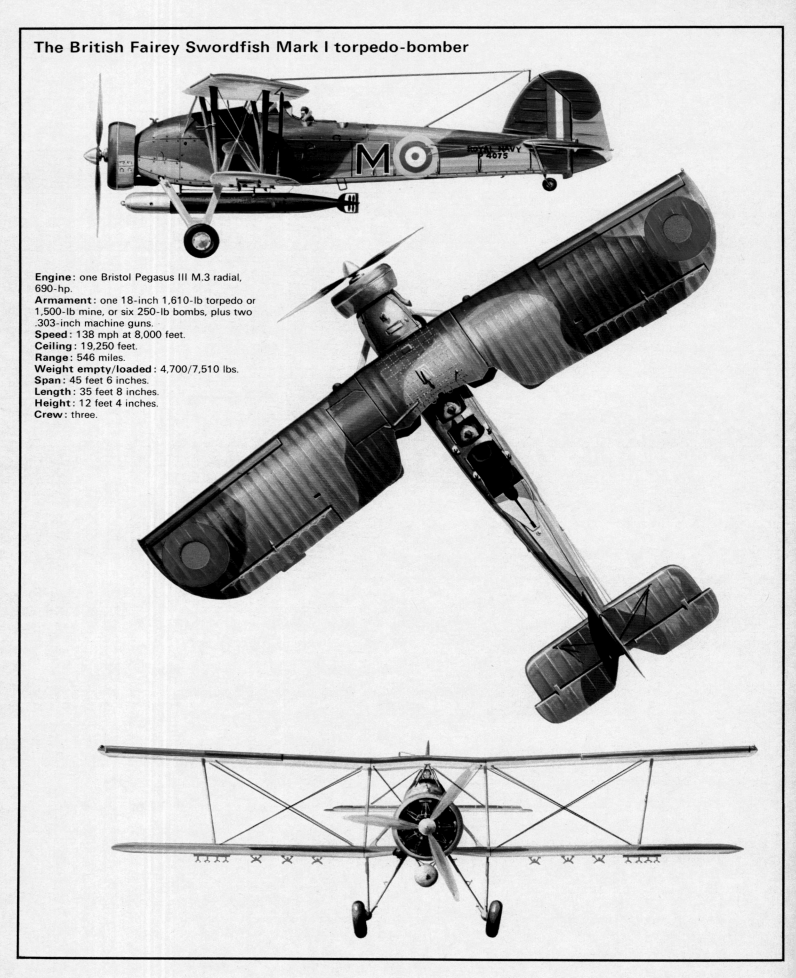

Engine: one Bristol Pegasus III M.3 radial, 690-hp.
Armament: one 18-inch 1,610-lb torpedo or 1,500-lb mine, or six 250-lb bombs, plus two .303-inch machine guns.
Speed: 138 mph at 8,000 feet.
Ceiling: 19,250 feet.
Range: 546 miles.
Weight empty/loaded: 4,700/7,510 lbs.
Span: 45 feet 6 inches.
Length: 35 feet 8 inches.
Height: 12 feet 4 inches.
Crew: three.

Mediterranean the battleship *Valiant* (fresh from a refit), the anti-aircraft cruisers *Calcutta* and *Coventry*, and, most important of all, the new aircraft-carrier *Illustrious*, which carried 34 aircraft, of which 12 were Fulmar fighters. With this reinforcement Cunningham's battle fleet could defend itself adequately against the Italian bombers. *Illustrious* and *Valiant* had the additional advantage of being equipped with radar.

Thus the Royal Navy had reacted promptly and skilfully: these new reinforcements anchored at Alexandria on September 5.

During the operation the veteran aircraft-carrier *Argus*, having steamed to the south of Sardinia, flew off 12 Hurricanes to strengthen the threadbare defences of Malta. It is surprising to note that after the neutralisation of Bizerta with the signing of the armistice, the Italians had made no attempt to take Malta. The defences of the "island fortress" were pitifully weak: there were only 68 light and heavy A.A. guns instead of the 156 guns which had been envisaged in a pre-war programme, and the one radar set on the island functioned only sporadically. When Italy entered the war on June 10 Malta's air defences consisted of five Swordfish torpedo-bombers and four Sea Gladiators; one of the latter was soon damaged beyond repair, and the remaining three were christened "Faith", "Hope", and "Charity". These were later joined by nine Swordfish and nine Hurricanes.

Admiral Cunningham had protested against the running-down of Malta's defences which the British Government and the Imperial General Staff had countenanced, but his complaints had not been taken up. London had decided that in the event of a war with Italy the Middle East theatre would be supplied by the sea route round the Cape of Good Hope. But in view of the timidity of *Comando Supremo* and the weaknesses of the Italian Air Force it was decided to restore to Malta the offensive rôle which had seemed impossible because of the menace of the bomber.

But to do this it would be necessary to proceed by very careful and easy stages while the defences of the island remained as weak as they were. Cunningham saw this very clearly. He wrote at the time: "If we are to avoid a serious threat to Malta itself, it appears necessary that in any given period the scale of attack drawn down should not be disproportionate to the state of the defences it has been possible

to install. It is only logical therefore to expect the full weight of Italian attack if our light forces work effectively."

In the long run, the offensive action of the light surface forces and the bombers which would be based on Malta would depend on the parallel development of Malta's defences (fighters, anti-aircraft guns, and radar). This was obvious; it was confirmed by experience. But it did not appeal to Churchill, who reproached Cunningham on September 9 for not being sufficiently offensively minded.

△ *The last minutes of the Italian cruiser* Bartolomeo Colleoni, *sunk on July 19. The Australian cruiser* Sydney *landed repeated hits on the* Colleoni *and wrecked her engine room. Dead in the water and defenceless, the* Colleoni *was finished off by torpedoes from the destroyers* Hyperion *and* Ilex.

Weary Italian troops on the Albanian front, where, thanks to the inefficiency of the Fascist régime, the Italian soldier "earned the martyr's crown a thousand times over".

CHAPTER 27
Albania, Sidi Barrani, Taranto

Meanwhile, a local conflict with no direct connection with the war between the major powers was about to become a matter of great importance. Soon it would impinge upon the joint interests of Germany and Italy—with fateful results.

We have already mentioned that neither the Hungarian Regent, Admiral Horthy, the various governments at Budapest, or Hungarian national opinion had accepted the territorial restrictions imposed upon Hungary by the Treaty of Trianon in 1920. After Munich, Hungary had obtained substantial frontier rectifications at the expense of Czechoslovakia; later, in March 1939, the Prague coup had enabled her to occupy and annex Sub-Carpathian Ruthenia. But Hungary had other claims to make, against both Yugoslavia and Rumania.

For many years the region of Transylvania had been a source of discord between Rumania and Hungary. With the defeat of Austria-Hungary in 1918, Hungary had been forced to cede Transylvania to Rumania, the latter country being one of the victorious Allies. It was a fair enough decision, considering that the majority of the population was Rumanian and that it had endured harsh treatment while under Hungarian rule. But along the bend of the Carpathians there was a compact bloc of Magyars, known as Szeklers or Sicules. There were around two million of them, and were cut off from their fellow Magyars on the Danubian plain. When they became Rumanian citizens, they had not reason to be pleased with their change of nationality.

△ *Admiral Horthy, Regent of Hungary, enters Navygarad in triumph.*
▽ *Ribbentrop talks with the Rumanian leaders Manoïlescu (centre) and Gafencu.*

The Axis verdict

After the crushing of France, the Hungarian Government once again raised the question of Transylvania. But although King Carol II of Rumania and his Prime Minister, Gigurtu, were prepared to consider certain concessions, no complete agreement between the rival countries seemed possible. They would have gone to war but for the intervention of Hitler, who, as we have seen, feared the consequences of any outbreak of trouble in the Balkans, and Mussolini, who always tended to favour the cause of the Hungarians. Rumania and Hungary submitted to Axis arbitration, which was presided over by Ciano and Ribbentrop in the Belvedere Palace in Vienna. On August 30, 1940, the Axis verdict was delivered.

Under the terms of the Axis arbitration, Rumania would retain the western part of Transylvania. Hungary recovered the region of the Szeklers, but in order to extend her 1920 frontier to the Moldavian Carpathians she was also granted territory occupied by some three million Rumanians, plus the important towns of Cluj and Oradea, which for the next four years were known by the Magyar names of Kolozsvar and Nagyvarad.

·This high-handed partition of Transylvania still did not satisfy the Hungarian claims in full. On the other hand, coming as it did two months after the loss of Bessarabia and the Bukovina to Soviet Russia, it sparked off deep feelings of resentment among the Rumanians. On September 4 General Ion Antonescu seized power, forced King Carol to abdicate in favour of his son Prince Michael, and, taking the title of "Conducator", set up a dictatorship.

German patronage for Rumania

As Italy, of the two Axis partners, had always supported Hungary's cause, it was not surprising that both King Carol and Antonescu had thought it advisable to seek German patronage. Hitler was extremely anxious not to be cut off from the output of the Rumanian oil wells at Ploieşti, and to safeguard them from possible Allied attempts at sabotage. As a result, he welcomed eagerly the request made to him by a Rumanian military mission which visited him on September 2. And on October 7, Lieutenant-General Hansen and his staff, together with the first elements of the 13th Motorised Division, arrived in Bucharest.

This move, coming as it did after the guarantee of territorial integrity which had been given to Rumania after the Vienna arbitration, could only be interpreted as a clear-cut anti-Soviet move by Hitler. Stalin and Molotov, however, showed no outward reaction. But the effect on Mussolini was totally different.

Mussolini turns on Greece

On October 12 Ciano visited Mussolini in the Palazzo Venezia. He found the Duce "indignant", claiming that the occupation of Rumania by German troops had had a very bad impression on Italian public opinion. He had made his decision. "Hitler always faces me with a *fait accompli*. This time I am going to pay him back in his own coin. He will find out from the papers that I have occupied Greece. In this way the equilibrium will be re-established."

No other decision of Mussolini's could have been more welcome to Ciano, who had always pressed for imperialist Italian policies in the eastern Mediterranean. Nevertheless he thought it necessary to ask if Mussolini had discussed the matter with Marshal Badoglio. "Not yet," he replied, "but I shall send in my resignation as an Italian if anyone objects to our fighting the Greeks."

On the 15th Badoglio and Roatta, appalled, heard of Mussolini's decision. Three weeks before, acting on his orders, they had demobilised 600,000 men. Now he was asking them to attack Greece within 12 days, D-Day being set as dawn on October 26.

Without objecting to the operation in principle, Badoglio undertook to attack with 20 Italian divisions on condition that the Bulgarians would undertake to tie down six to eight Greek divisions. But General Sebastiano Visconti-Prasca, commanding in Albania, only had eight Italian divisions under his orders. It would therefore be necessary to remobilise 12 more divisions, send them across the Adriatic, and set up the necessary depôts and reserves for them on the spot. Considering the inadequacies of the Albanian ports of

Valona and Durazzo, all this needed at least three months.

Mussolini could not accept these arguments: everything suggested that such a delay would allow Hitler to interpose a new veto. Ciano, Jacomoni (Lieutenant-General of Albania), and Visconti-Prasca all supported the idea. During the discussions on October 15 at the Palazzo Venezia they destroyed the objections of Badoglio and Roatta; and they were backed by Admiral Cavagnari and General Pricolo, respectively Under-Secretary of State and Chief-of-Staff of the Navy, and Chief-of-Staff of the Air Force.

As Ciano saw it, the political situation was favourable. Neither Turkey nor Yugoslavia would support Greece, their ally in the Balkan Pact, and Bulgaria's attitude would be favourable to Italy. But above all, the political situation in Athens gave cause for reasonable optimism. Only the Court and the plutocracy remained hostile to Fascist Italy, and a well-organised system of bribery was laying the groundwork for a change of régime.

For his part, Jacomoni claimed that the

entire population of Albania was anxious to settle accounts with Greece, its hereditary enemy. "One can even state," he declared proudly, "that the enthusiasm is so great that it [the Albanian people] has recently given signs of disillusionment that the war has not already begun." Asked to present his plan of operations, Visconti-Prasca declared that he foresaw no difficulty in opening the campaign with his current forces in Albania. Leaving a covering force on the Pindus Mountains on the eastern sector, he undertook to conquer Epirus in 10 to 15 days, throwing 70,000 Italians against 30,000 Greeks. Then, reinforced from Italy and from the Ionian Islands through the captured port of Préveza, he would march on Athens, whose fall would end the campaign before the close of the year.

Faced with these arguments, particularly the political explanations of Ciano and Jacomoni, Badoglio gave way. He contented himself with saying that the Peloponnese and Crete should be included as objectives, for otherwise the British would move in. He has been blamed –

correctly – for the exaggerated military promises which he made. But at the time he had no idea of the extent to which the claims of Ciano and Jacomoni were totally mistaken.

Nevertheless, Mussolini granted his generals a deadline extension of two days, and he impressed on all parties that the whole affair was to be kept a strict secret from the Germans.

Hitler and the Mediterranean

While the preliminary studies for an invasion of Soviet Russia were still under way, Hitler, on the urging of Grand Admiral Raeder and the suspension of Operation "Sea Lion", was showing signs of interest in a strategic project which could have lessened the weakening effects of the "parallel war" and allowed the Axis partners to co-operate more directly in their fight against the common enemy. This was Operation "Felix", aimed at the conquest of Gibraltar.

If the Wehrmacht could establish itself on the Strait of Gibraltar it could close the Mediterranean to the Royal Navy and give the Italian fleet access to the Atlantic. It would also enable the Axis to put French North Africa, where Weygand had just installed himself, under pressure similar to that already being imposed on Unoccupied France. It would no longer be possible for Vichy France to fend off Hitler's demands by pleading the possible defection of Morocco, Algeria, and Tunisia.

Overtures to Franco

Such an operation would require the co-operation of Spain. When it seemed likely that Hitler was about to invade Britain, the Spanish Government had raised the question of Spain's claims to Oran and the French zone of the Moroccan protectorate. In mid-September Serrano Suñer, Spanish Minister of the Interior and Franco's brother-in-law, met Hitler and Ribbentrop for a series of talks. According to his account, which, it is true, was written after the war, he was disappointed – not to say shaken – by the German reaction to these overtures.

▽ Hitler and General Franco meet at Hendaye, on the Spanish frontier. For once Hitler's magnetism failed completely: the Spanish dictator refused to join the Axis partnership.

Ciano's diary confirms Suñer's version. On October 1 it records "Serrano's colourful invectives against the Germans for their absolute lack of tact in dealing with Spain. Serrano is right." Hitler and Ribbentrop wanted the Atlantic coast of Morocco for Germany, plus an air and naval base in the Canary Isles. Moreover, they were still uncertain about the economic aid which Germany could send to would only impose further bitter sacrifices on the Spanish people.

As Hitler continued to speak in general terms, affirming that Britain was already beaten, Franco turned down the invitation to enter the war on the day that the Wehrmacht attacked Gibraltar, provisionally set for January 10, 1941.

Interpreter Paul Schmidt was an eyewitness at this discussion. "To put it

Spain, for the moment she entered the war Spain would instantly be cut off from her important imports of cereals and fuel, and would then become dependent on Germany.

On October 4 the same question was raised at the Brenner Pass conference between Hitler, Mussolini, Ribbentrop, and Ciano. At the same time the eventual dispatch of a German armoured detachment to North Africa was discussed. But Mussolini, who was still waiting from day to day for Graziani to resume his offensive in Egypt, cold-shouldered the idea. In his opinion, Panzer troops should only be sent to North Africa after the third phase of the operation: when the Italian 10th Army moved east from Marsa Matrûh on Alexandria and Cairo. There can be no doubt, however, that he hoped to be able to avoid German help.

Franco meets Hitler

If the Italians had taken Cairo by October 22, Franco could well have acted very differently. As it was, on that day he met Hitler at Hendaye on the Spanish frontier. Franco believed that the war would in fact be a long one and that without firm guarantees of corn and fuel supplies it

bluntly, I was most interested to hear Franco's reply to Hitler's declaration that from the jumping-off point of Gibraltar, Africa could be rid of the British by armoured troops." This was quite possible along the fringe of the great desert, said Franco, "but central Africa is protected against any large-scale land offensive by the desert belt, which defends it as the sea defends an island. I have fought a great deal in Africa and I am certain of it."

Schmidt's account continues: "Even Hitler's hopes of eventually conquering Britain might turn out to be hollow. Franco thought it possible that the British Isles could be conquered. But if this happened the British Government and fleet would carry on the struggle from Canada, with American aid.

"While Franco talked on in a calm, monotonous, sing-song voice like an Arabic muezzin, Hitler began to grow more and more restless. The discussion was clearly fraying his nerves. At one stage he even got up and said that further discussion would be useless, but he soon sat down and continued his attempt to change Franco's mind. Franco declared that he was prepared to conclude a treaty but, in view of the supplies of food and armaments Hitler was prepared to offer from the moment Spain went to war, that the offer was only a hollow sham."

△ *Another moral defeat for Hitler: his meeting with Pétain at Montoire on October 24, 1940. "Pétain listened in silence," recalled interpreter Schmidt. "Not once did he offer a single friendly word for Hitler or for Germany."*

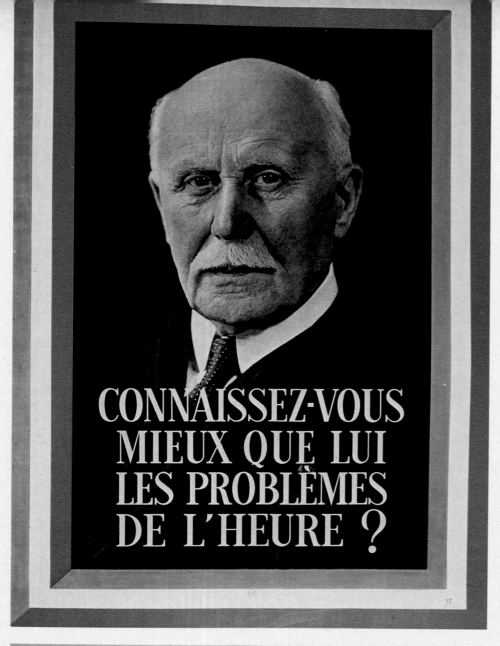

CONNAISSEZ-VOUS MIEUX QUE LUI LES PROBLÈMES DE L'HEURE ?

COLLABORATION

Comment on l'envisageait
après Montoire
entre la France et l'Allemagne

Ce qu'ils en ont fait

Finira-t-elle
ainsi ?

Franco was using the technique which can loosely be described as "yes, but", and it was not at all to the liking of Hitler. Ribbentrop, too, was receiving the same treatment from Serrano Suñer, who had only lately become the Spanish Minister of Foreign Affairs. Ribbentrop's latest proposal had not been well received by Suñer: "Spain will receive territories from the French colonial empire, for which France can be compensated in equal measure by territories from the British colonial empire."

This was very different to what had been said to Suñer during his visit to Berlin; but Ribbentrop, too, was infuriated by the caution of the Spaniards. Schmidt, who flew to Montoire with Ribbentrop, has described him as "fuming with rage", and spending the journey in invective against "that ungrateful rogue" Franco and "that Jesuit" Suñer.

Pétain checks Hitler

If Hitler's meeting with Franco at Hendaye was a definite setback for German policies, his meeting with Pétain at Montoire did nothing to compensate for it. Hitler wanted to induce the Vichy French Government to go to war with Britain. Pétain, however, left Hitler in no doubt as to his refusal to allow France to be drawn into a war with her former ally, even on the pretext of reconquering the colonies which had gone over to de Gaulle.

Once again, Schmidt has provided an account of the Montoire meeting.

"As darkness fell on October 24, 1940, it was difficult at first to tell the victor from the vanquished in the feeble lights on the platform of the little station. Standing very straight, despite his great age, in his plain uniform, Pétain put out his hand to the dictator with an almost royal gesture, while fixing him with a quizzical, icy, and penetrating glance. I knew how he felt about Hitler, Göring, and other prominent National Socialists. To most Germans he himself stood for all the military virtues of France, and this was very clear in Hitler's attitude when they met. He was no longer the triumphal victor shown by certain photographs of 1940. Nor was he a corporal intimidated in the presence of a marshal, as certain French publications have since claimed. He behaved without haughtiness and without harshness.

"With a gesture, Hitler invited the Marshal to enter his railway car. I myself was seated before Pétain and was admirably placed to observe him throughout the talk. His complexion, which had seemed pale to me on the platform, became faintly pink. No emotion or interior tension could be seen behind his mask of impassivity. Ribbentrop, a mute and almost tolerated witness, together with Laval, who was wearing his inevitable white tie, assisted the conversation.

"Pétain listened in silence. Not once did he offer a single friendly word for Hitler or for Germany.

"His attitude conveyed a vaguely haughty impression, rising above the situation of France in this autumn of 1940."

"Führer, we are on the march!"

But Hitler had hardly left Montoire when a message from the German Ambassador in Rome threw him into the deepest consternation: his ally was on the brink of invading Greece. In the hope of staving off this dangerous venture, he went straight to Italy instead of returning to Berlin. At 1000 hours on October 28, he was greeted at the station in Florence by Mussolini, all smiles, who announced: "Führer, we are on the march! At dawn this morning our Italian troops victoriously crossed the Albanian-Greek frontier!"

Koritsa, Taranto, and Sidi Barrani were three decisive defeats for Italian arms which severely darkened the prospects of the Axis. They gave the suppressed peoples of Western Europe their first glimmer of hope since June 25, 1940. From the moment the attack began, Mussolini and Ciano watched while the political assumptions on which the war with Greece had been founded began to collapse. They already knew that King Boris of Bulgaria would stay on the sidelines until events had run their course. They had grossly underestimated the patriotism of the Greek nation, which closed its ranks under the feeble Italian bombing raids when it heard that King George II and the Prime Minister, General Joannis Metaxas, had indignantly rejected the Italian ultimatum and had immediately decreed general mobilisation.

The fact was that Italy was violently unpopular in Greece. Quite apart from the historical legacy of the Venetian rule in Crete, the Morea, and the Ionian Islands, the Fascist methods brought to bear on the people of Rhodes and the Dodocanese by Count Cesare de Vecchi had resulted in the unanimous hostility of all sectors of Greek opinion against Mussolini, his régime, and his country.

◁△ Vichy propaganda boosting Pétain. "Do you know more than he does about the problems of the hour?"
◁▽ German propaganda for the benefit of French collaborators, warning that subversive Jewish activities could well wreck the Franco-German agreement reached at Montoire.
△ Mussolini's march on Athens begins: Italian troops cross into Greece over a pontoon bridge.

The Greeks hit back

General mobilisation gave the Greek commander, General Alexandros Papagos, 15 infantry divisions, four infantry brigades, and a cavalry division, formed into five army corps. On paper the Greek divisions were definitely inferior to the Italian divisions, but this disparity was largely balanced by the chronic difficulties

1 2

3 4

358

of the terrain and of communications, which favoured the defenders.

In the Italian plan the initial assault would be carried out by four divisions attacking in Epirus, with another two divisions covering the main attack by advancing against the Morova massif. Visconti-Prasca planned a breakthrough which would surprise Papagos before he could concentrate his forces. But the weather was on the side of the Greeks: the Italians crossed the frontier in torrential rain which converted every brook into a torrent and every road into a sea of clinging mud. In these conditions the demolitions carried out by the Greeks added still further to the slowing-up of the Italian advance.

Nevertheless, Visconti-Prasca's left-hand column, formed by the "Julia" Alpine Division, broke through the advanced Greek positions, then their main position, pushed up the Aóos valley and took the village of Vovoússa on November 2. Here the division found itself at the foot of the important Métzovon pass, crossed by the Lárisa–Yanina road, having covered some 25 miles of mountain terrain under an icy rain. On the following day a Greek counter-attack down from the

In the autumn of 1940 there was world-wide speculation as to the outcome of Italy's ventures in the Balkans and North Africa; and Axis, Allied, and neutral cartoonists each had their own interpretations of the pattern of events. 1. *The king of the desert beats a hasty retreat:* Berlin's Lustige Blätter *exults over Britain's withdrawal from British Somaliland, effected in the face of overpowering Italian pressure in August.* 2. *Inevitably, the British were foremost in poking fun at Mussolini's bellicose ambitions. Here* Punch *depicts a cowering Duce as gasping "At last! The British fleet!" as the British camel corps advances.* 3. *The* San Francisco Chronicle *underlines a fact which the Wehrmacht's victories in Poland, Scandinavia, and the West had made quite obvious: Germany's dominance in the Axis partnership.* 4. *Another dig at Britain's forces in North Africa by* Lustige Blätter: *the desert army is on such short rations that the men are forced to eat their prematurely-prepared victor's laurels.* 5. *A neat summing up of Mussolini's dilemma in September 1940 by Stockholm's* Der Svenska Bildtidningen.
Hitler: "Well, Benito, so you're going to move, eh?"
Mussolini: "Sure . . . but which barrel do I jump into, Egypt or Greece?"
6. *As had happened when the Soviet Union attacked Finland in December 1939, the free world rang with applause when the Greeks not only stood up to Italy's invasion but won victory after victory over the Duce's armies. This cartoon, by* Punch, *is entitled, quite simply, "Trophies of the mountains".*

In the coastal sector, the "Siena" Division was luckier. It took Filiates crossed the raging River Thíamis, and reached Paramithia with the intention of encircling the Greek position at Yanina. At sea, appalling conditions forced *Comando Supremo* to abandon its projected amphibious operation against Corfu, while bad weather prevented the Italian Air Force from bringing its superiority to bear.

The Italians had lost all the advantage of surprise: the Italian bombers were not able to slow down the mobilisation and concentration of the Greek forces; and all the weaknesses of the plan adopted on the recommendation of Visconti-Prasca were now obvious. By November 12 General Papagos had at the front over 100 infantry battalions fighting in terrain to which they were accustomed, compared with less than 50 Italian battalions.

Visconti-Prasca was dismissed on November 9 and was replaced by General Ubaldo Soddu, Under-Secretary of State for War and Deputy Chief-of-Staff of the Army. He now found two armies under his command: on the right, General Carlo Gelosa's 11th Army, and on the left General Mario Vercellino's 9th Army. But until the remobilised divisions could be shipped across the Adriatic these units were armies only in name.

On the Greek side, General Papagos did not content himself with the success of his defensive strategy; in this war, with 45 million Italians attacking seven million

△ *Greek soldiers–incredibly tough, with a fighting spirit second to none.*
▽ *An Italian motorcyclist in difficulties; Torrential rain converted the primitive roads of Albania into quagmires.*
▽▷ *Italian transport halts beside a road which has been mashed to a swamp by the wheels of previous vehicles after the torrential November rains.*

heights forced the Italians into a retreat that was as hasty as it was disastrous.

In the centre, the 23rd "Ferrana" Infantry Division and the 131st "Centauro" Armoured Division, which had Yanina as their first objective, were held up by the Greek forward positions and completely halted by their main position, largely as a result of the action fought by the Greek 8th Division, acting as covering force.

Greeks, a "wait and see" policy would have been tantamount to an admission of defeat. Papagos determined to exploit the errors committed by the Italians and to counter-attack before the enormous numerical and material superiority of the Italian Army could be brought into play. On November 14 the Greek Army went over to the offensive along the entire front from Lake Prespa to the sea.

On the Greek right, V Corps under General Tzolakoglou, fielding at first three and finally five divisions, broke through at Mount Morova and after eight days' fighting had destroyed the Italian 9th Army at Koritsa, taking 2,000 prisoners, 80 field guns, 55 anti-tank guns and 300 machine guns from the "Tridentina" Mountain Division and the "Arezzo", "Parma", and "Piemonte" Infantry Divisions. This brilliant success was exploited further to the north, and on December 4 the Greek III Corps occupied Pogradec on Lake Ohrida.

On November 21 the II Corps under General Papadopoulos also crossed the Albanian frontier, despite the formidable obstacle of the Grámmos massif, and took Ersekë and Leskovik. This gave the Greek High Command an excellent front between the Koritsa plateau and the valley of the Aóos. On December 5, a gallant action gave the II Corps Përmet, 23 miles inside Albania. On the left, the I Corps under General Kosmas crossed the Thíamis on the heels of the retreating 11th Army. Pushing down the Dhrin valley, the Greek advance guards were greeted enthusiastically by the population of Argyrokastron – which says much for the deep Albanian feelings of loyalty towards Italy which Jacomoni had described to Mussolini. Two days before, the left-flank division under General Kosmas had taken Sarandë, formerly Santi Quaranta, which the Italian Fascist régime had rechristened Porto Edda.

After December 5 the Greek offensive began to peter out. The Greek Army's lack of tanks and its poverty in anti-tank weapons forced it to shun the plains and valleys in its attacks, and so the excellent Greek infantrymen concentrated on the mountain heights for their operations. But by the beginning of December temperatures in the mountains were falling as low as 15 and even 20 degrees Centigrade below zero, and these were rendered even more unbearable by severe snowstorms.

Lacking tanks, lacking even sufficient transport vehicles, the Greeks now began

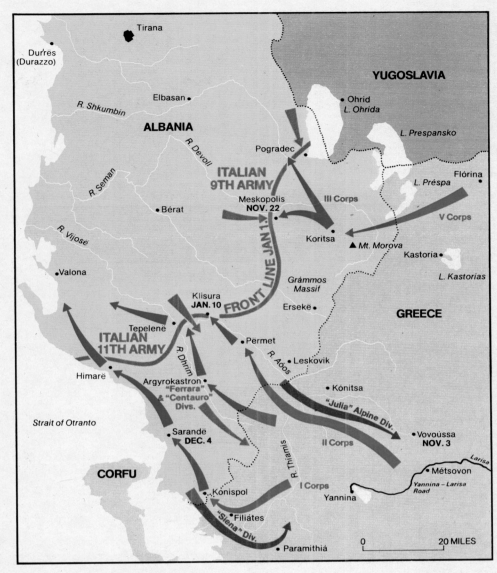

to experience the sufferings of their enemy. The British had no material which they could spare for their new allies. On the other hand, no less than eight Italian divisions had been shipped to Albania between October 28 and the end of December. Far too often, however, the demands of the front led General Soddu to use up his reinforcements piecemeal to plug local breakthroughs. But quite apart from this, the supply of Italian reinforcements was badly organised.

However, the comparatively rapid supply of Italian reinforcements only raised fresh problems with regard to their supplies. On December 4 the Quartermaster-General, Scuero, described the depôt and magazine supplies as almost completely exhausted.

No one could deny the victor's laurels to the Greek soldier. But under conditions like these one can only say that the Italian soldier had earned the martyr's crown a thousand times over.

△ *The Italian invasion of Greece and the Greek counter-attacks. The Greek commander, General Papagos, timed his counter-stroke perfectly.*
▽ *The Italian commander in Albania: General Soddu. He liked to spend his evenings with his somewhat unmilitary hobby of composing music for films.*

△ △ *Mainstay of the Italian bomber arm: the Savoia-Marchetti S.M.-79, unattractive but effective.*
△ *Italian Air Force briefing photograph for bombing raids on Malta, with the key forts, gun batteries, arsenals, reservoirs, and fuel dumps all carefully identified and numbered. Malta's vital airfields at Hal Far and Luqa are at the top right of the picture, numbered 24 and 25.*

Taranto

Meanwhile, the British Mediterranean Fleet had struck as deadly a blow as the Greek Army. From the moment when the aircraft-carrier *Illustrious* joined his command, Cunningham detected a certain lack of offensive spirit in the Italian squadron based on Taranto. This led to

the preparation of a British torpedo-bombing attack: Operation "Judgement".

The first idea of Rear-Admiral Lyster, commanding the British carrier force in the Mediterranean, had been to attack on the night of October 21, the anniversary of Trafalgar; but an accident aboard *Illustrious* forced him to postpone "Judgement" until November 11, when the phase of the moon would next favour the venture. Then he had to operate without the aircraft-carrier *Eagle*, which transferred some of her Swordfish aircraft to *Illustrious*, however. Despite all this, Cunningham put to sea on November 6 to co-operate with a sortie by Force H, which was escorting the battleship *Barham* on its journey to the eastern Mediterranean.

On the evening of November 11 an air reconnaissance from Malta carried out by Martin Marylands and Short Sunderlands established that all six of the Italian battleships were in port. Having steamed to within 190 miles of Taranto, Lyster flew off his 21 Swordfish in two waves. Eleven of them were fitted with torpedoes and the other ten with bombs and flares.

Several circumstances favoured the attackers. A few days before, a heavy storm had driven down several balloons from the barrage protecting the Taranto anchorage. The anti-torpedo nets surrounding the warships only extended 26 feet down while the British torpedoes, set to detonate either on contact or by magnetic proximity, ran at 30 feet. Finally, when the alert was sounded, the Italians did not activate the harbour smoke-screens, in order not to impair the fire of the anti-aircraft guns. Nevertheless, the Fleet Air Arm crews needed all their dash and gallantry to penetrate the fire of the 21 100-mm batteries and the 200 light A.A. guns, quite apart from the guns aboard the warships, mark their targets, and drop their torpedoes accurately.

Eleven torpedoes were launched, and six scored hits: three on the *Littorio*, two on the *Duilio*, and one on the *Cavour*. The last Swordfish returned to *Illustrious* at about 0300 hours. The British lost only two aircraft. In reply, the Italian land batteries alone had fired some 8,500 shells. Of the aircraft crews, one was killed and three others were taken prisoner. *Littorio* and *Duilio* were out of action for the next six months and needed considerable repairs. The older *Cavour* was raised, towed from Taranto to Trieste, and abandoned there. Until the summer of 1941 *Supermarina*'s battle fleet was reduced to three battleships, which permitted Admiral Cunningham to release the elderly British battleships *Ramillies* and *Malaya* for much-needed escort duties on the Atlantic convoy routes.

This series of disasters caused near chaos in the Italian High Command. Refusing to put the blame where it belonged – on his own vanity – Mussolini decided to make a scapegoat of Marshal Badoglio. But as the Commander-in-Chief of the

Italian Armed Forces could hardly level a public indictment against his own Chief of General Staff, Mussolini opened his campaign against Badoglio with a vicious editorial aimed at the Marshal by Roberto Farinacci, editor of the official paper *Regime Fascista*. Badoglio demanded a public retraction of this allegation that he was not only incompetent but had also betrayed Mussolini's trust by ignorance or deliberate treachery. When he was refused all satisfaction, Badoglio resigned on November 26.

General Ugo Cavallero stepped into his place. Apart from the torrent of defamation poured on his character in Ciano's diary, it must be said that Cavallero was a much-discussed figure among his fellow

generals, and that a period of involvement in the arms industry had not added to his prestige. Admiral Cavagnari was dismissed as head of *Supermarina* and Under-Secretary of State for the Navy and was replaced by Admiral Arturo Riccardi, a fact which publicly branded the former as the man responsible for the Taranto fiasco. Finally, de Vecchi resigned and was replaced by General Ettore Bastico as Governor of the Aegean.

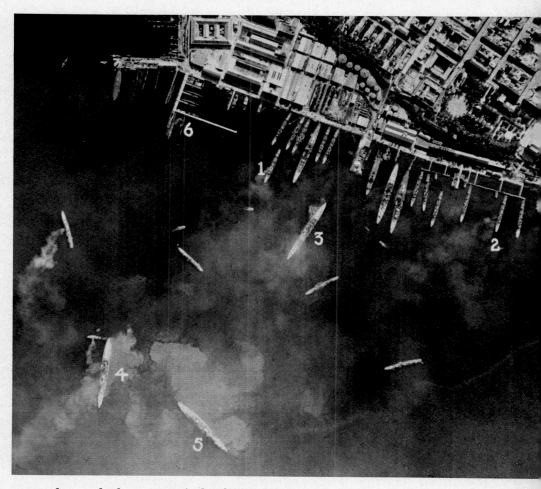

▽ *Aftermath of the Taranto raid: a reconnaissance photograph of the inner harbour, where the cruisers were anchored, on the day after the raid. Oil fuel lies thick on the water; a tug fusses about the stern of a Bolzano-class heavy cruiser (4). The other crippled heavy cruiser (5) belongs to the* Trento *class. A second* Trento-*class vessel (3). has been moved from the quayside. The three large ships still moored by the quay are Zara-class heavy cruisers, which escaped without damage. In the outer harbour, the battleships* Littorio *and* Caio Duilio *were put out of action for six months, and the* Cavour *so badly damaged that she never put to sea again:*

△ "Taranto" by Bagley. A dramatic reconstruction of the action that wrested numerical superiority from the Italian Navy at the end of 1941.

Although Hitler was infuriated by the disasters which his friend and ally had brought down on himself, the interests of the Reich nevertheless made it essential for the Wehrmacht to retrieve the situation. On November 18, at the Berghof, Hitler made himself clear to Ciano: he had only sent German troops into Rumania to safeguard the Ploieşti oil wells from Soviet machinations, and now they would be within range of R.A.F. bombers if the British set up air bases in Greece. He therefore proposed to invade Greece via Bulgaria, and set the provisional date at around March 15.

But this new plan of Hitler's meant that Mussolini must reverse his entire policy towards Yugoslavia. Instead of the aggressive attitude which Mussolini had always kept up, it was now essential to bring Yugoslavia into the Axis. Ciano, however, had reservations about the political decisions which governed Hitler's military intervention in the Balkans. It was clear to him that from now on Italy would not be waging a war aimed at her own interests, and that the future relations between Mussolini and Hitler would be those of vassal and lord.

The day after Ciano's departure from Berchtesgaden, Hitler and Ribbentrop put their cards on the table before the Spanish Foreign Minister, Serrano Suñer. On November 12 Hitler had ordered the preliminary moves for Operation "Felix", which was to capture Gibraltar. It was vital to waste no further time in establishing Franco's final intentions.

Suñer restated the arguments which had been put forward at Hendaye. The capture of Gibraltar, he declared, would not pay full dividends until the Italians had taken Port Said, the key to the other entrance to the Mediterranean. Moreover, Spain would need nearly 400,000 tons of cereals and two months to prepare for war. For all his powers of persuasion, Hitler failed to get Suñer to modify this point of view. Suñer left the Berghof without having accepted anything, but – and this was probably even more important – without having issued a flat refusal.

The Italian defeats at Koritsa and Taranto had certainly done much to influence Franco's decision. In less than a month, the further defeat at Sidi Barrani would confirm the Caudillo in his policy of non-belligerence.

CHAPTER 28
Attack in the Desert

▽ *The British tracked maid-of-all-work underwent numerous changes of designation during its service career, but was most commonly known merely as the "Bren-gun carrier"*

In December 1940 Wavell not only abandoned the defensive to which he had been confined since June 25, but launched an offensive which won such a total success that Hitler was forced to send yet more German forces to help his tottering ally, now facing ruin only six months after his entry into the war. Wavell was also helped immeasurably in that his opponent Graziani made a considerable contribution to the defeat of his own forces.

Certain aspects of this episode would still be unknown were it not for the surprising information contained in the memoirs of Sir Anthony Eden. He was secretary of State for War at the time, and what he has to say on the preparation for Wavell's attack on Sidi Barrani throws a very different light on the story told by Churchill's *The Second World War*.

"A good average colonel and would make a good chairman of a Tory association." That was how Churchill described Wavell after a visit by the latter to London between August 8–15, 1940. Worse still, he did not feel in him, as he wrote to Eden, "the sense of mental vigour and resolve to overcome obstacles, which was indispensable to successful war." Moreover, Churchill's readiness to scrutinise Wavell's dispositions, "to move this battalion here and that battalion there." left Wavell "clearly upset". He even considered offering his resignation.

In *The Second World War* Churchill chose to play down this clash, in which he was proved utterly wrong by the course of events. But whatever one thinks of Churchill's account, written years after the event, nothing can detract from the heroic decision he made at the time. Thirty days before the invasion which was anticipated for mid-September 1940, it was decided to weaken the British Home Forces in order to reinforce Wavell's command in Egypt.

In all there were three tank battalions (154 armoured vehicles), 48 anti-tank guns, 48 25-pounder field guns, and other infantry weapons which Churchill wanted to send to Egypt through the Mediterranean. As the Admiralty refused to accept responsibility, the risk being too great, these reinforcements were sent out round the Cape. On September 19 they entered

The British Carrier, Universal Number 1, Mark II

Weight: 4¼ tons.
Crew: 4.
Armament: one .55-inch Boys anti-tank rifle, two .303-inch Bren machine guns, and one 2-inch mortar.
Armour: 7-mm minimum, 10-mm maximum.
Engine: Ford V-8, 85-hp. **Speed:** 30 mph. **Range:** 160 miles.
Length: 12 feet 4 inches. **Width:** 6 feet 11 inches. **Height:** 5 feet 3 inches.

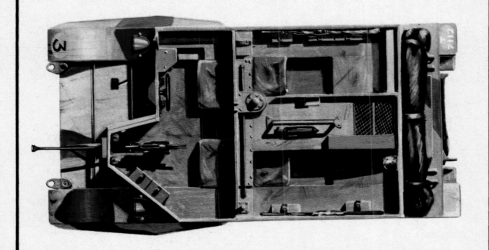

the Red Sea, finding no challenge from the Italian naval forces based on Massawa. The British air forces in the Middle East were also being reinforced. Between the end of August and the end of December 1940, 107 Hurricane fighters and Blenheim bombers were taken by sea to Takoradi on the Gold Coast and flown across Africa by devious stages to Khartoum on the Nile. When French Equatorial Africa, and particularly the important staging-post of Fort Lamy, went over to de Gaulle's cause, it became possible to build up the Takoradi air route into a key supply line.

Wavell's opportunities

"What would happen if the Italians were not to attack?" asked Eden on October 15, when he visited Wavell in Cairo. By way of reply Wavell brought in General Sir Henry Maitland Wilson, commanding the British forces in Egypt, and asked him to explain to Eden the plan of attack – or

rather of strategic envelopment – whic had been prepared against the Italia forces dug in at Sidi Barrani.

At this time, it should be noted th Italian attack on Greece had led to mor tension between London and G.H.Q. Cair The British War Cabinet demanded effe tive aid for the Greeks; and very u willingly, as their own resources wer weak, Wavell and Air Chief-Marshal Si Arthur Longmore, Air Officer Comman ing Mediterranean and Middle Eas agreed to send 63 fighters and 46 bomber to Greece in two months.

There was equal friction and conflict interests between Rome and Tripol Mussolini was pressing Graziani to marc on Marsa Matrûh without further delay while Graziani wanted to wait until he ha been supplied with three more motorise battalions, with armoured cars, and wit water trucks. Exasperated, Mussolin warned Graziani on October 21 that if an further objections were raised he woul not hesitate to accept Graziani's resigna tion. Nothing came of this, doubtles because of the catastrophe on the Greek front.

The Greek venture and its disastrous results for Italy rebounded as far as the Western Desert, for the emergency transport of supplies to the Albanian front which it necessitated cut down the reserves of mobile forces which might reasonably have been sent to North Africa before the resumption of the campaign. Thus Mussolini's share of the blame for the defeat of December 9 was great, but it did not excuse the mistakes of Graziani, Berti, and Gariboldi.

Battle at Sidi Barrani

The Italian forces around Sidi Barrani had severe weaknesses in their deployment. In the first line, General Gallina's Libyan Corps held the 19 miles between Maktila on the coast and Nibeiwa in the desert. In reserve, General Merzari's "3rd of January" Black Shirt Division, occupying Sidi Barrani itself, was some 12 miles back from the units which it would be required to support. In the second line, XXI Corps (General Dalmazzo) had its "Cirene" Division dug in on the escarpment, 20 miles west of Nibeiwa. The area between the two points was patrolled only weakly.

Such a strung-out disposition was fatally vulnerable to an armoured attack. As it could not be adjusted within 24 hours it exposed the Italian Army, "motorised on foot", as a wag referred to it, to piecemeal destruction. In addition, the rocky terrain had prevented an anti-tank ditch from being dug, and there were not enough mines and too few 47-mm anti-tank guns to repel an armoured advance.

Matters were worsened by Italian Intelligence's failure to grasp British plans. Graziani believed that the British were over 200,000 strong – a wildly exaggerated figure. But it did not prevent him giving permission for General Berti to go to Italy at the end of November. At the front, there was the impression that something was afoot, but the increase in British motorised patrols had not caused the Italians to change their dispositions before December 9.

By then it was too late. At dawn on the 9th, surging forward from their concentration-point in the desert (which had been christened "Piccadilly Circus") the British 7th Armoured Division and 4th Indian Division struck through the gap in

The British Rolls-Royce Armoured Car
1920 Pattern Mark I

Weight: 3.8 tons.
Armament: one .303-inch Vickers machine gun (most Western Desert vehicles had an open-topped turret fitted with a Boys anti-tank rifle, a Bren gun, and a smoke discharger).
Armour: 9-mm.
Engine: 50-hp Rolls-Royce.
Speed: 45 mph.
Range: 180 miles.
Length: 16 feet 7 inches.
Width: 6 feet 3 inches.
Height: 7 feet 7 inches.
Crew: three.

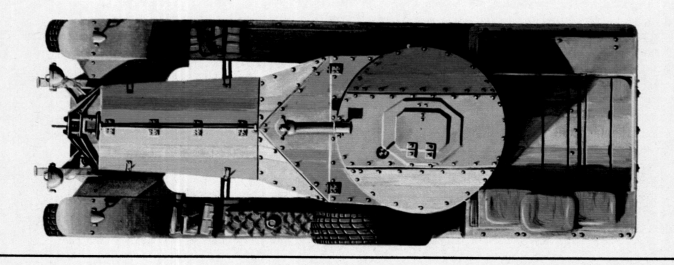

the Italian front, while a brigade under Brigadier A. R. Selby attacked Maktila on the coast road. The entire force, soon to be known as XIII Corps, was under the command of Lieutenant-General Richard O'Connor, and consisted of only 36,000 men and 225 armoured vehicles; among the latter were 57 Infantry tanks known as "Matildas", whose massive armour was proof against the Italian shells.

The 4th Indian Division and the Matilda tank battalion attacked Nibeiwa, which was defended by the Maletti Motorised Group. Surprise was complete, for the uproar of the artillery and air bombardment drowned the noise of engines and tank tracks, and the British were attacking from the south-west and even from the west. Badly wounded, General Maletti fought on until he was killed at the head of his troops, but by 0830 it was all over. For the price of 56 dead, Major-General Beresford-Peirse, commanding 4th Indian Division, had taken 2,000 prisoners.

Encamped at Tummar, General Pescatori of the 2nd Libyan Division planned to march to the sound of the guns as soon as the British attack began. But 4th Indian Division and the Matildas saved him the trouble. Thrown back, Pescatori counterattacked with spirit, but his forces were broken up by crushing British artillery fire. Tummar West fell in the afternoon while Tummar East did not surrender until dawn on the 10th.

In the evening of December 9, Brigadier J. A. L. Caunter's 7th Armoured Division reached the sea, cutting off the retreat of the survivors of the 2nd Libyan Division. Facing Sidi Barrani, Selby Force had thrown General Sibille's 1st Libyan Division (not without some trouble) out of its position at Maktila. The Italian pocket thus formed at Maktila was cleaned up with the assistance of British naval bombardment, a task which had been completed by the evening of the 11th.

During the same day Graziani ordered XXI Corps to fall back immediately to the Halfaya–Sollum–Capuzzo line on the frontier. The "Cirene" Division got the order in time and fell back without trouble. But this was not the case with General Spinelli's "Catanzaro" Division, thanks to an error in transmission. It was caught on the move between Buqbuq and Sollum and half annihilated.

This last defeat raised the losses of the Italian 10th Army to 38,000 prisoners, 237 guns, and 73 tanks, while the British losses amounted to only 624 killed, wounded, and missing. But O'Connor's

▽ *The end of the line for some of the 38,000 Italian 10th Army prisoners "put into the bag" in the first stage of Wavell's offensive towards Libya, as they are marched through Cairo under British escort.*

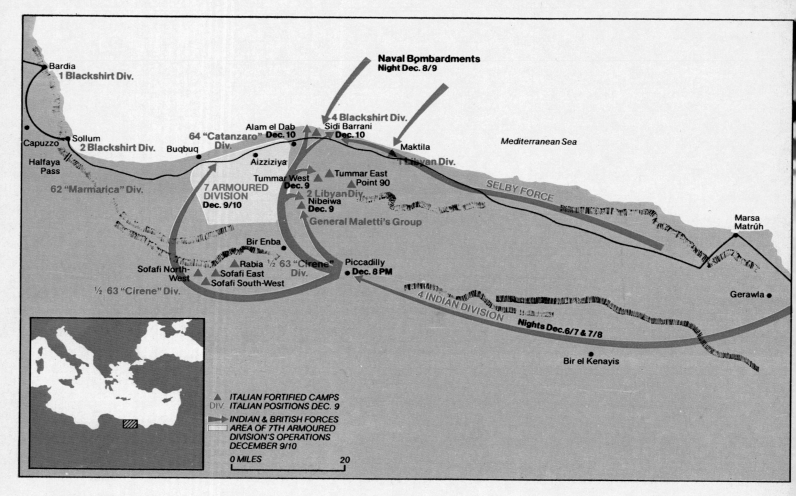

Map labels:

Bardia
1 Blackshirt Div.
Naval Bombardments
Night Dec. 8/9
4 Blackshirt Div.
Sidi Barrani Dec. 10
Mediterranean Sea
Capuzzo
Sollum
2 Blackshirt Div.
Buqbuq
64 "Catanzaro" Div.
Alam el Dab Dec. 10
Aizziziya
Maktila
1 Libyan Div.
Halfaya Pass
62 "Marmarica" Div.
7 ARMOURED DIVISION Dec. 9/10
Tummar West Dec. 9
Tummar East
Point 90
2 Libyan Div.
Nibeiwa Dec. 9
SELBY FORCE
Marsa Matrûh
General Maletti's Group
Bir Enba
Sofafi North-West
Rabia ½ 63 "Cirene" Div.
Sofafi East
Sofafi South-West
½ 63 "Cirene" Div.
Piccadilly Dec. 8 PM
4 INDIAN DIVISION
Nights Dec. 6/7 & 7/8
Gerawla
Bir el Kenayis

▲ ITALIAN FORTIFIED CAMPS
DIV. ITALIAN POSITIONS DEC. 9
INDIAN & BRITISH FORCES
AREA OF 7TH ARMOURED DIVISION'S OPERATIONS DECEMBER 9/10
0 MILES 20

△ *The unexpected counter-stroke: Wavell's surprise attack, which took the Italian defences of Sidi Barrani in flank and left the British poised for a deep thrust into the Italian colony of Libya.*

force had no sooner won this glorious and virtually painless victory than it was seriously weakened by the withdrawal of the excellent 4th Indian Division, which was earmarked for the campaign against the Italians in Eritrea.

It is now clear that this was a mistake. In Italian East Africa the Duke of Aosta, Viceroy of Abyssinia, was already so weak that the Anglo-Egyptian Sudan had nothing to fear from his forces, and the same applied to Kenya. The 4th Indian Division was badly missed in the Western Desert.

Was Wavell to blame? Certainly, the original scope of Operation "Compass", the attack on the Italians at Sidi Barrani, was limited to a five-day raid after which O'Connor was to fall back on Marsa Matrûh. But the real responsibility lay much higher. The British War Cabinet was deeply concerned with Abyssinia, and Churchill was at the same time trying to interest the Imperial General Staff in a venture called Operation "Workshop", directed against the Italian island of Pantelleria in the Mediterranean.

The 6th Australian Division (Major-General I. G. Mackay) replaced 4th Indian Division in XIII Corps. But General

O'Connor did not wait for its arrival before launching an all-out pursuit against the beaten and disorganised Italian forces. On December 14 he crossed the frontier south of Capuzzo, swung his armoured and motorised forces to the north, and invested Bardia on the 18th. The Bardia perimeter, 24 miles in extent, was defended by General Bergonzoli's XXIII Corps, with the survivors of the "Catanzaro" and "Cirene" Divisions from Egypt, General Tracchia's "Marmarica" Division, and General Antonelli's "23rd of March" Black Shirt Division – a total force of 45,000 men and 430 guns.

On December 18, General Mackay's 6th Australian Division joined XIII Corps. Prospects for the Axis darkened with the fall of Bardia right at the beginning of 1941; not even the first major fire raid on London on the night of December 30–31 did much to redress the balance. In the occupied or threatened countries of Europe there was a widespread feeling that the defeat of Mussolini would only be a matter of time, and that that of Hitler would follow.

But in view of the military weakness of Great Britain and her Empire, this was very far from the truth . . .

◁ *The hunter prepares: a look-out on the bridge of a German U-boat scans the horizon for signs of a British convoy.*

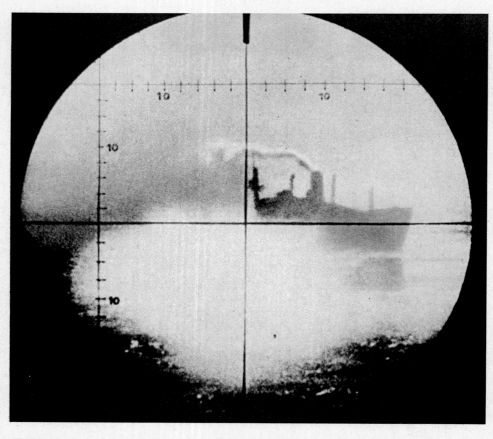

During the first three months of 1940 the course of the war at sea caused the French and the British little concern. The handful of U-boats at the disposal of Admiral Dönitz had scored only mediocre success against the Allied convoys, which had been organised at the outbreak of the war. Including neutral vessels, only 108 merchantmen totalling 343,610 tons were sunk by U-boats between January 1 and March 31, 1940, and the building capacity of the British shipyards alone was estimated at 200,000 tons per month. In the same period no less than eight U-boats were sunk by Allied naval escorts, though one was subsequently salved. It was therefore not surprising that at the beginning of April the French and British Admiralties had no worries about the immediate future.

Looking further ahead, the French and the British were well aware that U-boat activity would increase, thanks to the construction capacity of the shipyards on the Baltic and the North Sea. But at the same time the war programmes of the two Western powers were also beginning to bear fruit, and the strength of the convoy escorts was growing in parallel with increased U-boat production. Admiral of the Fleet Sir Dudley Pound and Admiral Darlan believed that they had the situation well in hand.

Already the dangerous effects of the magnetic mine, which was impervious to traditional mine-sweeping techniques, had been overcome. But in November 1939 the magnetic mine had come as a very disagreeable shock; in that month alone 27 ships – 120,958 tons in all – had been sunk by mines. Once the secret of the magnetic mine had been pierced, however, the French and the British began intense "degaussing" work on their ships. The results of this counter-move were soon apparent. In March 1940 losses to mines had fallen to 14 ships totalling 35,501 tons.

In the South Atlantic the Battle of the River Plate on December 13, 1939, had put a stop to the modest exploits of the pocket-battleship *Graf Spee*, which by that date had sunk 50,081 tons of shipping. The month before, on November 15, *Graf Spee*'s sister ship *Deutschland* had dropped anchor in Gotenhafen (formerly Gdynia) after a ten-week war cruise in the North Atlantic which had brought her little gain: only two victims, a total of 7,000 tons. Since then no German surface raider had broken out through the Royal Navy's blockade line between Iceland and the Orkneys.

Germany's "torpedo scandal"

On March 4, 1940, at the moment when he was preparing to send eight U-boats into the North Atlantic and six to the North Sea, Admiral Dönitz was ordered to refrain temporarily from any new operations. It was necessary for the U-boats to participate in *Weserübung*, the invasion of Scandinavia. Their task was to destroy Allied warships which tried to attack the German convoys heading for Norway, while also attacking and destroying the troopships which the Allies, once they had recovered from their intial surprise, were certain to send to the support of the Norwegians in the Trondheim and Narvik regions.

No less than 31 U-boats were involved in this new mission, which meant that during April–May 1940 Germany's submarine commerce-raiding was virtually suspended. According to the figures in *The War at Sea*, the British official history, total Allied and neutral mercantile losses during the Norwegian campaign amounted to only 20 ships totalling little more than 88,000 tons – the lowest losses to U-boats since the outbreak of hostilities.

This was a considerable setback for the German Navy and it was not compensated for by almost total failure in Norwegian waters. There were plenty of tempting targets for the U-boats; their crews were not lacking in courage or training. But their torpedoes, despite reports made during the previous autumn and official promises, were still chronically unreliable.

In reviewing the logs of the U-boats in action between April 11 and 19, Admiral Dönitz was presented with the following depressing account of the failures recorded by his boats:

"April 11:

"Launched torpedoes at two destroyers at 10 in the evening. Result not observed. [*U-25*].

"At 1230 hours, launched three torpedoes at the *Cumberland*. Miss: explosion at the end of the run. At 2115 hours, launched three torpedoes at a *York*-class cruiser. Premature explosions. Depth 23 feet; Zone 4. [*U-48*].

"April 10, 2250 hours: Two failures: an explosion after 330 yards, another after 30 seconds, 110 yards short of a big destroyer. [*U-51*].

◁ △ *A British freighter, viewed through the periscope of a German U-boat as a torpedo streaks towards it.* ◁▽ *The end for a similar British vessel. But with the help of the Allies and captured shipping, Britain was able to replace most of the shipping lost to the U-boats–so far.* △ *The wolves rest: part of a U-boat flotilla tied up in its home port.* ◁ *The wolves prepare: The crew slides a torpedo down onto its rack in the torpedo room in the bows of a U-boat.*

"April 15:
"On the 14th, fired without success at the *Warspite* and two destroyers. [*U-48*]. Launched two torpedoes at a transport. Failures. [*U-65*].
"April 18:
"Two premature explosions between Iceland and the Shetlands. [*U-37*].
"April 19:
"Launched two torpedoes at the *Warspite*, at 980 yards. Depth 26 feet, zone 4. A premature explosion and a terminated run. [*U-47*].
"Fired at the cruiser *Emerald*, at the mouth of Vaagsfjord. Premature explosion after 22 seconds. [*U-65*]."

On April 16 Commander Günther Prien in *U-47*, the "hero of Scapa Flow", was on patrol in the Byddenfjord when he surprised a convoy at anchor – a solid wall of shipping. He fired eight torpedoes, all of which failed. On returning from his cruise he told his superiors "that it was useless to send him to fight with a dummy rifle".

In 1940 the magnetic detonator used in the German torpedo had not come up to expectations. It was not a unique problem: the British suffered from the same trouble in 1941 and the Americans in 1942. The percussion detonator was also found to be useless as the torpedoes ran some 10 feet below the depth for which they had been designed, with the result that they often passed harmlessly beneath the keel of the target.

According to Dönitz, the defective German torpedoes spared an entire British squadron – the battleship *Warspite*, seven cruisers, seven destroyers and five transports. What was worse, the premature explosions of the torpedoes gave away the presence of the U-boats and resulted in violent counter-attacks. Six U-boats were sunk in the North Sea between April 10 and May 31.

After Norway: return of the U-boats

In June 1940 the German victory in Norway allowed Dönitz to resume U-boat commerce raiding in the Atlantic. A rapid score of 58 ships sunk (284,113 tons in all) beat the best U-boat record over the last three months. Moreover, from airfields in Holland, Belgium, and northern France, the Luftwaffe was much better placed to attack British shipping in the Channel, either by direct attack or by mine-laying operations, which between them inflicted losses of 44 ships (191,269 tons). The total losses – caused by all forms of Axis attack by sea and air – amounted to 140 merchant ships (585,496 tons) sunk by the end of June.

The intervention of Italy and the French surrender reversed the entire naval strategic situation in favour of Germany. To challenge the Italians in the Western Mediterranean, formerly the responsibility of Admiral Darlan and the French fleet, now fell to the British Force H, ordinarily composed of one aircraft-carrier and one or two battleships or

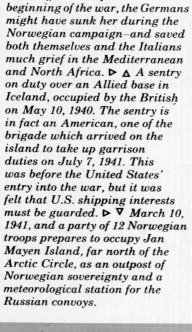

▽ *The battleship* Warspite. *Given efficient torpedoes at the beginning of the war, the Germans might have sunk her during the Norwegian campaign–and saved both themselves and the Italians much grief in the Mediterranean and North Africa.* ▷ △ *A sentry on duty over an Allied base in Iceland, occupied by the British on May 10, 1940. The sentry is in fact an American, one of the brigade which arrived on the island to take up garrison duties on July 7, 1941. This was before the United States' entry into the war, but it was felt that U.S. shipping interests must be guarded.* ▷ ▽ *March 10, 1941, and a party of 12 Norwegian troops prepares to occupy Jan Mayen Island, far north of the Arctic Circle, as an outpost of Norwegian sovereignty and a meteorological station for the Russian convoys.*

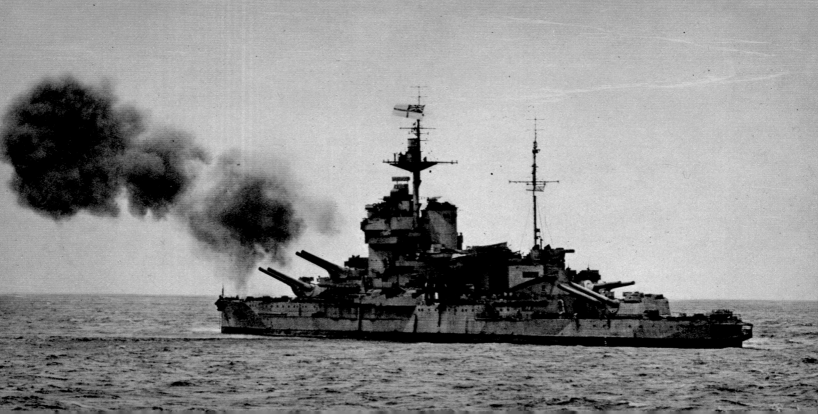

battle-cruisers, based on Gibraltar. The entire British naval strength in the Mediterranean between Gibraltar and Alexandria amounted to one-third of the capital ships in service with the Royal Navy.

With the exception of the warships which fled for British ports at the time of the French capitulation, about 60 French destroyers and torpedo-boats had been removed from the board and would no longer be able to assist in convoy escort duties as the German submarine offensive took shape again. Despite the attacks of the Luftwaffe, the British shipyards were producing an enormous number of destroyers and corvettes designed specifically for anti-U-boat warfare, but it would be some time before they entered service.

Above all else, the Third Reich had just acquired an enormous strategic advantage for its Navy, which would permit the most varied selection of strategic combinations. At the end of 1914 Colonel-General von Falkenhayn – had he not been halted on the Yser and in front of Ypres – would have been satisfied to provide the Imperial German Navy with the ports of Dunkirk, Calais, and Boulogne. By the end of June 1940 Grand-Admiral Raeder could dispose of every Atlantic port between Tromsö and St. Jean-de-Luz.

It was true that the ports between Rotterdam and Cherbourg were too close to the British air bases to be of service to more than the most lightweight German naval forces. But in this sector the Luftwaffe could stand in for the German Navy. During July 1940 the German bombers sank four destroyers and 18 small merchantmen. German air attacks became so serious that the coal suppliers of Cardiff were told to ship their consignments for the London region via Scotland.

Germany's Navy: all advantage, no strength

In his work on the story of German naval strategy in the two world wars, Vice-Admiral Kurt Assmann wrote significantly of the situation of the German Navy after the conquest of Norway and the French surrender:

"At this time the situation was the reverse of that of 1914. Then we had been in possession of a navy which could tackle the British Grand Fleet on its own terms,

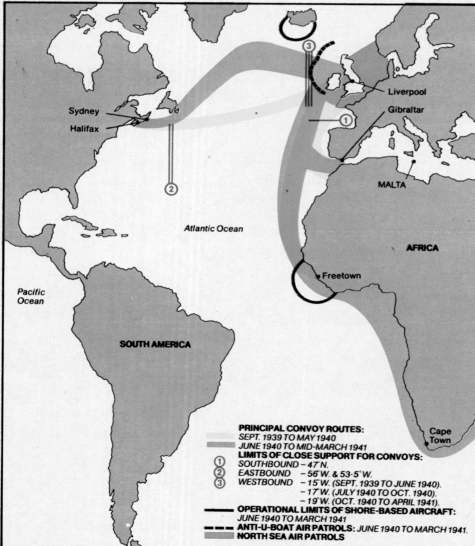

PRINCIPAL CONVOY ROUTES:
SEPT. 1939 TO MAY 1940
JUNE 1940 TO MID-MARCH 1941
LIMITS OF CLOSE SUPPORT FOR CONVOYS:
① SOUTHBOUND – 47°N.
② EASTBOUND – 56°W. & 53.5°W.
③ WESTBOUND – 15°W. (SEPT. 1939 TO JUNE 1940).
– 17°W. (JULY 1940 TO OCT. 1940).
– 19°W. (OCT. 1940 TO APRIL 1941).
OPERATIONAL LIMITS OF SHORE-BASED AIRCRAFT:
JUNE 1940 TO MARCH 1941
ANTI-U-BOAT AIR PATROLS: JUNE 1940 TO MARCH 1941.
NORTH SEA AIR PATROLS

but which had no strategic advantage with regard to its bases. Now we had this strategic advantage, but we had no fleet strong enough to exploit it.

"Moreover, in this new situation, because of the circumstances of World War II we were threatened from the sky, for our bases lay within range of the British air forces, which had not been the case in 1914. From this point of view the British had a distinct advantage over us. The Home Fleet anchorages in northern Scotland were over twice as far away from the German air bases – even those in Norway – than the new German bases in France were from the airfields of the Royal Air Force."

These comments revive a question which has been asked before. What would have happened if Hitler, having modified his policies to suit the "Z-Plan" ship-building programme (which under Raeder's direction would have given him a powerful surface fleet and 300 U-boats), had gained in 1946 the same strategic advantages that he did in 1940? It is a sobering thought, particularly as there is no way of knowing what counter-measures the French and the British would have taken in the intervening years.

Despite the naval situation created by the German invasion of Norway and the conquest of France, however, Britain's position was not as bad as is often imagined.

After the German invasion of Denmark,

Britain had proceeded to occupy the former Danish territories of the Faeroe Islands and Iceland on May 10, 1940. Shortly afterwards the British Admiralty set up a naval base at Hvalfjord on the western coast of Iceland, just to the north of Reykjavik. Although it was now unable to blockade the northern exit to the North Sea by controlling the waters between Scapa Flow and Stavanger, the Royal Navy still held the North Atlantic approaches along the line Orkneys–Shetlands–Faeroes–Iceland–Greenland.

The invasion of Norway and of Holland, and the installation in Britain of the Norwegian and Dutch Governments in exile headed by King Haakon and Queen Wilhelmina, put at the disposal of the British all the Norwegian and Dutch merchantmen which the Germans had not surprised in their home ports. This came to about one-third of the strength of the British Merchant Navy at the outbreak of hostilities. In addition, there were the officers and men of the Norwegian and Dutch Navies, like their Polish comrades, whether aboard ships of their own which they had managed to save from disaster or aboard destroyers, escorts, or even submarines which the British High Command put at their disposal. Finally, at the time of the armistice and for some time afterwards, the British took over all the French merchantmen they could get, in port or at sea.

Given these reinforcements, it was with some 28 or even 30 million tons of shipping that Britain faced the Battle of the Atlantic, instead of the 21 million which she had had in September 1939. Another advantage came from the fact that Britain was now released, as a result of the German victory, from the obligation to help supply her French ally.

The convoy system

The installation of the German Air Force and Navy in the French bases on the Channel and the Atlantic led the British Admiralty to route the North American convoys further to the north. Convoys for Freetown, the first or last stage on the Cape of Good Hope route, were sent further to the west. Ships sailing to or from Liverpool now took the North Channel between Ireland and Scotland instead of St. George's Channel, the latter being judged too dangerous. But these detours meant that a convoy steaming at 10 knots would take 15 days to reach Britain from New York, while a convoy steaming at $7\frac{1}{2}$ knots would take 19 days to make the passage from Freetown.

New headquarters and commander

During the first phase of the Battle of the Atlantic the defence of the Western Approaches against U-boat and Luftwaffe attacks had been entrusted to Admiral Sir M. Dunbar-Nasmith, V.C., C.-in-C. Western Approaches, with his H.Q. at Plymouth. Soon afterwards, however, the Western Approaches H.Q. – on which the successful outcome of the war depended – was transferred to Liverpool, and was taken over by Admiral Sir Percy Noble on February 17, 1941.

Dönitz – wizard of the U-boat war

Across the Channel Admiral Dönitz, high priest of the German U-boat theory and strategy, was not long in seizing the considerable (if not decisive) advantages which the German victories of May–June 1940 had given him.

As the passage of the Channel was closed to them, the U-boats had to reach their hunting-grounds in the North Atlan-

△ Admiral Sir Percy Noble, Commander-in-Chief, Western Approaches. With his headquarters in Liverpool, Noble was in an excellent position to co-ordinate the efforts of the Royal and Merchant Navies, and thus ensure that cargoes essential to Britain's physical survival, and well as her continuance in the war, reached their destination from America and the Empire.

◁△ A German coastal U-boat, employed mostly on Britain's east coast and in the Channel to disrupt the traffic in such bulk cargoes as coal. ◁▽ The Atlantic convoy routes, so vital to the survival of Great Britain as a fighting force. The danger spot, as can easily be seen, was the gap between the limits to which the escorts at either end of the routes could steam. Between these points the wolf packs had almost complete freedom of action. △ Part of defeated Europe's vital contribution: Dutch minesweepers off Britain.

SWEEPING THE SEAS

. The crew of a destroyer prepares to lower a paravane. Sweeping along at the end of its cable to one side of and behind its towing point, the paravane was designed to cut the mooring line of any mine it came to, causing the mine to float to the surface, where it could be disposed of by gun-fire. . The crew of a 20-mm Oerlikon cannon, an essential part of any minesweeping team: cannon fire was particularly effective for detonating the mines that had floated up to the surface after their wires had been cut, and was also invaluable in defence against air attack. **3.** Though their primary task was the defeat of the mine menace, the great fleet of British mine-sweepers was also ready to take on submarines, the other underwater threat. The minesweeper in this picture has its paravanes at the stern to deal with the one, and depth-charges the other. **4.** Its indicator flag flying bravely, a paravane buoy moments before being hoisted out. **5.** Typical of the hundreds of fishing vessels requisitioned by the Admiralty and converted into minesweepers: the *Reboundo* of 278 tons, an ex-trawler built in 1920. She was requisitioned in September 1939 and served right through the war, being returned to her owners in December 1945.

tic by making the long and dangerous northward voyage around the Orkneys, and this limited their operational period considerably. But if they could be based on the French Atlantic ports they would be spared an out-and-return voyage of over 1,000 miles, which would permit them to remain at large for an extra week.

German H.Q. moves

The armistice with France had not yet come into force when Dönitz made his first tour of the western ports, and decided to install himself at Lorient. On July 7, *U-30* became the first German submarine to use the port, taking on fuel and new torpedoes there. From August 3 teams of workers and specialists arrived from Germany to overhaul the port installations and make all the necessary alterations which would be needed by U-boats returning from the high seas. At the same time plans were drawn up for enormous pens in which U-boats would be protected from Allied bombs by 23 feet of concrete. Instead of concentrating on fruitless attempts to knock out the German shipyards, as it did in 1941 and 1942, the R.A.F. would have been better advised to try to destroy the huge U-boat pens before they were completed .

At the end of August 1940, Dönitz finally left his H.Q. at Wilhelmshaven and moved to Kernével, on the outskirts of Lorient. Together with his normal staff, Dönitz brought with him a large team of specialists of all kinds, with sophisticated electronic equipment.

There were radio direction-finding experts, trained to pinpoint the briefest signal sent out by Allied convoys; and decoding experts, who deciphered (without much trouble, it would appear) signals sent from mid-ocean, as well as instructions from the British Western Approaches command. With this kind of information, Dönitz's H.Q. could use powerful radio transmitters to pass information to the U-boats on patrol and direct them to their targets.

What high-quality radio communication had done for the Germans on land, permitting them to campaign with mass tank formations, was about to transform the German U-boat arm. From the H.Q. at Kernével, Dönitz could send out orders and deploy his U-boats not as isolated warships but as hunting packs.

"Wolf-pack" tactics

The group attack was the great German innovation in submarine tactics; it had not been used in World War I. The Germans called it *Rudeltaktik* or "pack tactics". To the British the U-boat concentrations were "wolf packs".

Another innovation was that instead of attacking by day from a submerged position, the U-boats now began to attack at night and on the surface. It was not as risky as it sounds: in the darkness, the low silhouette of a U-boat was hard to spot from the higher vantage point of a ship's deck, and movement on the surface was not picked up by the asdic detectors aboard the escorts. An improved percussion detonator, hastily developed, meant that German torpedoes now functioned better than before.

Although Dönitz, as Captain Roskill points out in *The War at Sea*, had revealed these new tactics in a book published just before the war in 1939, the British were surprised by the new turn in the sub-

Admiral of the Fleet Sir Dudley Pound was born in 1877 and entered the navy through H.M.S. *Britannia*. He served in the Grand Fleet in World War I, and as the Director of the Admiralty Plans Division (1922–25) before becoming Chief-of-Staff to Sir Roger Keyes (1925–27). He was promoted Rear-Admiral in 1926. From 1927 to 1929 he was Assistant Chief of Naval Staff and then Rear-Admiral Battle-Cruiser Squadron until 1931. Pound was promoted Vice-Admiral in 1930, and was 2nd Sea Lord from 1932 to 1935, when he was promoted Admiral. From 1936 to 1939 he was Commander-in-Chief, Mediterranean Fleet, and succeeded Sir Roger Backhouse as 1st Sea Lord in 1939, in which year he was promoted to Admiral of the Fleet. He died in 1943.

◁ *The new breed: a* Hunt-*class escort depth-charges a U-boat.*

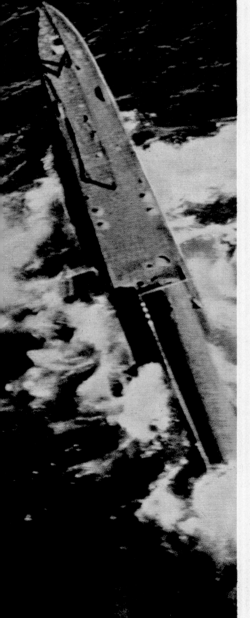

▽ The Italian submarine Gondar, *a coastal boat, which was sunk off Alexandria on September 30, 1940 by the British destroyer* Diamond, *the Australian destroyer* Stuart, *and aircraft of No. 230 Squadron – just one of the 20 submarines lost by the Italian Navy in its seven months of war in 1940.*

marine offensive and reacted sluggishly. These are the overall figures of British, Allied, and neutral tonnage sunk by U-boats in the second half of 1940:

 July – 38 ships (195,825 tons);
 August – 56 ships (267,618 tons);
 September – 59 ships (295,335 tons);
 October – 63 ships (352,407 tons);
 November – 32 ships (146,613 tons);
 December – 37 ships (212,590 tons);
 Total – 285 ships (1,470,388 tons).

The U-boat zenith

These successes were all the more remarkable in that they were obtained with quite small forces. On September 1, 1940, the German submarine arm had 57 U-boats, exactly the same number as at the outbreak of hostilities twelve months before, which showed that German U-boat construction had managed to compensate for the number of U-boats sunk: 28 in all. Because of the need for training, of the long trial periods before new U-boats were fit for operations, and the time taken up by U-boats in transit, there were never more than eight or nine U-boats operating simultaneously in the waters to the northwest of Ireland. But even more than with R.A.F. Fighter Command, quality counted for more than quantity.

Under picked commanders who had been selected during the numerous peacetime U-boat exercises – leaders such as Prien, Schepke, Kretschmer, Endrass, Frauenheim, and Oehrn – by October 1940 Dönitz's force had reached a level of proficiency which it was never to recover in World War II: 920 tons of shipping per U-boat sunk every day. The blockade of the British Isles, decreed on August 17, 1940, was no empty German boast.

A typical example is the tragic story of Convoys S.C.7 (34 merchantmen) and H.X.79 (49 ships), one sailing from Sydney, and the other from Halifax, Nova Scotia. In four nights – October 16–20 – six U-boats, attacking on the surface, sank 32 cargo-ships and tankers and damaged four others. The log-book of *U-99*, commanded by top-scoring U-boat ace Otto Kretschmer, tells a vivid story:

"October 18. 2330 hours. Now I attack the head of the right-hand column. Fire bow torpedo at a large freighter. As the ship turns towards us, the torpedo passes ahead of her and hits an even larger ship after a run of 1,740 metres. This ship of

7,000 tons is hit abreast the foremast and the bow quickly sinks below the surface, as two holds are apparently flooded.

"2355 hours. Fire bow torpedo at a large freighter of 6,000 tons at a range of 750 metres. Hit abreast foremast. Immediately after the torpedo explosion there is another explosion, with a high column of flame from bow to bridge. Smoke rises 200 metres. Bow apparently shattered.

Ship continues to burn with green flames.

"October 19. 0015 hours. Three destroyers approach the ship and search area in line abreast. I make off at full speed to the south-east, but soon regain contact with the convoy. Torpedoes from other submarines are constantly heard exploding. The destroyers do not know how to help and occupy themselves by constantly firing starshells which are of little effect in the bright moonlight. I now start attacking the convoy from astern.

"0138 hours. Fire bow torpedo at a deeply-laden freighter of about 6,000 tons. Distance 945 metres. Hit abreast foremast. The ship sinks with the explosion.

"0155 hours. Fire bow torpedo at the next ship, of about 7,000 tons. Distance 975 metres. Hit abreast foremast. It sinks in under 40 seconds."

△ *The apparent chaos of a German U-boat yard. During 1940, such yards turned out a monthly average of four boats. The production schedule envisaged by the "Z-Plan" was considerably higher. Luckily for the British, Göring's desire to boost provision for the Luftwaffe starved the yards of the necessary men and materials.*

The escort famine

In the period when each of Britain's leaders went to bed wondering if they would be awoken by the news of a German invasion, the number of escorts which could be spared for the convoys remained very small. Worse still, the old destroyers dating from World War I which were given the task had been designed for service in the North Sea, and lacked endurance. Incapable of refuelling at sea, they could not venture beyond Longitude 15 West from British ports, while the destroyers escorting east-bound convoys, based on Halifax, could not pass Longitude 35.

Until the new Icelandic base at Hval-fjord was completed there could be no question of filling the "Atlantic gap", as it was called, with the Coastal Command aircraft under Air Chief-Marshal Sir Frederick Bowhill. Coastal Command could put only 226 aircraft a day into the air in September 1940, and reinforcements arrived only in dribs and drabs as top priority was being given to Bomber Command, for an air offensive which was to prove futile in 1941.

The British were not helped by the personal intervention of Churchill, both as First Lord of the Admiralty during the "Phoney War" and afterwards as Prime Minister. Captain Donald Macintyre (a prominent U-boat hunter who had the honour of capturing Otto Kretschmer in March 1941) pulls no punches in his book *The Battle of the Atlantic*, quoting a plea for more offensive tactics which Churchill sent to Sir Dudley Pound at the end of 1939:

"Nothing can be more important in the anti-submarine war than to try to obtain an independent flotilla which could work like a cavalry division on the approaches, without worrying about the traffic or the U-boat sinkings, but could search large areas over a wide front. In this way these areas would become untenable to U-boats."

"A basic error," comments Macintyre, "which is to recur again and again in strategic thought on the Battle of the Atlantic, is here revealed. At nearly all stages of the Battle, the U-boat proved itself almost immune to surface or airborne search, except in the vicinity of convoys where, the area to be searched being greatly reduced, the submarine could either be kept submerged and so prevented from working its way in to the attack or, if surfaced in order to do so, could be detected and attacked."

The mistake, Macintyre stresses, was to detach escorts which were already too thin on the ground "to hunt U-boats reported perhaps 100 miles or more from the convoys. Search for a mouse reported in a ten-acre field had as much chance of success as these 'offensive' moves."

It was around the convoys themselves that the defenders had the best chance of making contact with U-boats, neutralising them by forcing them to dive, and then attacking and destroying them. So it was that the defensive tactics which Churchill deplored were in fact the best offensive methods possible.

Churchill asks for destroyers

Despite this fact, Britain's naval resources would remain over-stretched until the anti-submarine vessels ordered in the 1939 and 1940 programmes entered service. For this reason, Churchill turned to President Roosevelt, asking as early as May 15, 1940, for the cession of 40 or 50 American destroyers which had been built at the end of World War I. This request was repeated on July 11, as no reply had been received from the White House or the State Department.

It was obvious that any such concession would be in complete breach of the international conventions governing the relations of neutral states with belligerent ones. Although the majority of American public opinion was sympathetic to Britain and applauded her determination to fight on, it was also concerned about the reprisals which such a gesture might provoke from Hitler and Mussolini. In military circles there was also much apprehension that the "great arsenal of the democracies" might find herself involved in war before her production was fully prepared. Such was the level to which Roosevelt's "New Deal" policy had lowered the defensive capacity of the country.

Blending firmness with an admirable sense of compromise, Roosevelt replied to Churchill's request with a counter-proposal which would add to the military security of the United States. In exchange for 50 old destroyers, Great Britain would permit the U.S.A. to set up and occupy

bases in Guiana, the Antilles, Bermuda, the Bahamas, and, with the agreement of Canada, in Newfoundland, for a period of 99 years. London accepted these conditions with good grace; as Roskill points out in *The War at Sea*, they placed the defence of these scattered British possessions in the hands of American forces.

However, friction rapidly arose when Roosevelt sought to base the entire transaction on a formal declaration by the

◁ ◁ The war in the Atlantic: a convoy seen from the bridge of an ex-American World War I vintage destroyer, part of the "bases for destroyers" deal (top); the view across the columns of a convoy from an A.A. position (centre); and a U-boat hastening towards a convoy at speed on the surface. △ British destroyers in line ahead. Pre-war parsimony in such craft nearly brought Britain to the brink of defeat.

△ *Propaganda from occupied France about the British blockade: "His last hope . . . 'the blockade'. Will France have enough for them both?"* ▷ *Comment on British priorities from* Simplicissimus: *"You're drunk again, Father! Another British ship loaded with whisky must have been sunk."*

▷ △ *The weapon that failed to live up to expectations—the Focke Wulf Condor, which could have guided the U-boats right to their targets.* ▷ ▽ *German minesweepers at work clearing British mines from the French coast.*

British Government that the British fleet would be sailed to America if it could not be maintained in home waters. Although time was vital, Churchill tried to quash this request. It was not that he wished to make the Royal Navy a bargaining-point in case of an invasion, as some authorities have alleged, but that he was displeased that there should be any doubt at all about the matter. However, as Roosevelt continued to press the point, Churchill made Britain's attitude perfectly clear in the following letter, which he sent on August 31:

"You ask, Mr. President, whether my statement in Parliament on June 4, 1940, about Great Britain never surrendering or scuttling her Fleet 'represents the settled policy of His Majesty's Government'. It certainly does. I must however observe that these hypothetical contingencies seem more likely to concern the German Fleet, or what is left of it, than our own."

Fearing the worst

It seems clear that Roosevelt, without impugning the good faith or the resolution of the British, was wondering whether Britain's known weaknesses in armaments would result in her suffering the fate of Norway, Holland, Belgium, and France. If this were to happen it would be better if the Home Fleet left Scapa Flow before the Panzers arrived at Cape Wrath in the far north of Scotland . . .

Seven of the 50 American destroyers were sent to the Canadian Navy; two were manned by Norwegian crews. But even before they entered service, after having been fitted with asdic, the situation improved for the British. The R.A.F. had detected that the concentrations of barges in the invasion ports were being dispersed; and this permitted the Admiralty to divert to the Western Approaches command many destroyers which had hitherto been earmarked for operations against a German invasion fleet in the Narrow Seas.

A good example of how the struggle between the destroyers and the U-boats now began to turn in Britain's favour dates from March 15, 1941: the destruction of ace U-boat commander Joachim Schepke and his *U-100*, described by E. Romat in his *Atlantic Submarine War:*

"Badly damaged, *U-100* sank to the enormous depth of 750 feet. Schepke had

o other alternative than to surface. The
wo hunters grouped themselves so as to
ecover contact. *Vanoc*'s radar operator
eported a contact to starboard, and
lmost simultaneously her look-outs
potted a U-boat on the surface 540 yards
way. With a violent helm alteration the
estroyer wheeled round to starboard,
earing down on the U-boat. Schepke was
n bad trouble: his diesel engines had
ailed and he was running on his electric
notors; he could not make his intended
orpedo attack against the destroyer, as
e lacked the time and speed to reposition
is U-boat.

"The threatening bow drove closer and
loser. Schepke yelled to his crew to
bandon ship. Every man rushed onto the
ridge, putting on his lifebelt. At 1318
ours *Vanoc*'s bow rammed *U-100* almost
t right angles to the conning-tower,
licing through the pressure hull and
rushing Schepke to a pulp against the
ase of the periscope standards."

Britain would have had much more
rouble in fighting the menace of the
erman maritime blockade if Hitler and
öring had not reduced the German Navy
o the lowly status of Cinderella of the
erman armed forces.

▷ *The French steamer* Rouen, *impressed into German service as the naval auxiliary* Wullen- werrer. ▽ *A whaling factory ship, loaded with 22,000 tons of whale oil, arrives in Bordeaux after being captured by the* Pinguin, *one of Germany's most successful disguised raiders.* ▷▷ *A German warship lies idle at her moorings, a constant threat to the British Merchant Navy, but one which was seldom given the chance to test her strength.* ▷ ▽ *Another German warship, this time loose in the Atlantic on a commerce-raiding cruise.*

The wrong decision

When war broke out it had been decided to abandon the whole "Z-Plan" and concentrate naval construction on the completion of the battleships *Bismarck* and *Tirpitz*, the heavy cruisers *Prinz Eugen* and *Seydlitz*, the aircraft-carrier *Graf Zeppelin*, and above all the output of U-boats which, in about a year, were to enter service at the rate of 29 a month. According to German Navy calculations, the whole revised programme would not absorb more than five per cent of German steel production.

But when Hitler gave this order in October 1939 he left its execution to Göring, chief of armaments production, labour, and raw materials. But in his other capacity as head of the Luftwaffe Göring was unassailable, and the Navy got only the crumbs which fell from his table. By March 1940 Grand-Admiral Raeder had to accept a drop of monthly U-boat production from 29 to 25. But worse was to come. He had hoped that the land victories of the Wehrmacht would result in large industrial gains for the Navy; but nothing came of these hopes, for with the preparation first of Operation "Sea Lion" and then of "Barbarossa" his plans were ruined again.

As a result, the monthly U-boat production fell to two during the first half of 1940

nd struggled up to six during the second. n 1941 it grew from six to 13, and in 1942 rom 13 to 20 – but this last figure marked he limit, because of the fatal effects which he failure of the invasion of Russia had n German industry. Roskill was certainly ight when he stated: "The slowness with vhich the Germans expanded their U-boat onstruction was to have the most fortu- ate consequences for Britain."

The influence which Göring exerted on litler had equally damaging effects on he success of the U-boat offensive. Everything that flies is my concern," vas his boast. As a result, compared with he systems in use in Britain, the United tates, and Japan, the German Navy was enied the fleet air arm which it should ave had, and was dependent upon the ood humour of Göring for the collabora- ion (always improvised, at best) of the ierman air forces. As in Italy, this system f an "autonomous air arm" failed as soon s it was applied to the realities of modern aval warfare.

As case in point was the tragic accident f February 22, 1940, when two German estroyers were lost in the North Sea: eberecht Maass under Stuka bombard- ent, and *Max Schultz*, which only scaped the bombs of the Stukas by head- ng into a minefield, with fatal results.

The transfer of the U-boats to the French oasts seemed to offer brilliant oppor- unities to the Luftwaffe; by flying perma- ent patrols in the skies over the Western

△ *The crew of the* Sunbeam II, *a tug, prepares to recover a German mine entangled in the paravane line of the minesweeper* Selkirk, *the first such operation undertaken by the British, in August 1940. After the* Sunbeam *has hauled the* Selkirk's *gear on board, the mine and its sinker are disconnected, the latter is pulled on board the tug, and the former taken in tow to Harwich for examination.*
▽ *The far-ranging operational areas of the disguised German raiders, from the Atlantic to the Pacific and even Antarctica.*

Approaches German aircraft could have kept in contact with the Allied convoys, alerted the "wolf packs", and directed them to their targets. But the essential peacetime training for this rôle was lacking, and pilots were often nearly 100 miles in error in the reports which they made to Kernéval. Moreover, the codes which they used did not allow them to communicate with the operational U-boats directly.

Raeder and Dönitz tried in vain to give Hitler a better understanding of the problem. One can only sympathise with Dönitz when he declared to Hitler, one day in 1943: "The historians will describe World War II in different ways, according to their nationality. On one point, however, they will be unanimous. In the 20th Century – that of the aeroplane – the German Navy fought without airborne information and without its own air force, as if the aeroplane did not exist. And they will be unable to explain it."

We should remember Hitler's own description of the three branches of the Wehrmacht: "I have a National Socialist Air Force, a reactionary Army, and a Christian Navy!" Given this frame of mind it was hardly surprising that Göring's opinions tended to prevail over those of the admirals.

The German surface raiders

The German surface ships, too, played an important part in the campaign against Britain's sealanes. At the end of October 1940 the pocket-battleship *Admiral Scheer* broke out into the Atlantic and began a commerce-raiding cruise which took her to the Indian Ocean. On March 30, 1941, having returned via the Denmark Strait between Greenland and Iceland, she returned safely to the Baltic.

Even more spectacular were the succes-

ses of the disguised merchant raiders in service with the German Navy. They were fast merchant ships equipped with multiple camouflage devices, which enabled them to pass themselves off as Soviet ships in Norwegian waters, Spanish in the central Atlantic, and Dutch or Japanese in the Pacific. Carefully concealed, their armament normally consisted of six 5·9-inch guns, four torpedo-tubes, and a seaplane, plus around 100 mines, which these dangerous raiders sowed off the Cape of Good Hope and Australian and New Zealand ports.

Between March 31 and December 3, 1940, six of these disguised merchant raiders sailed from German ports. Among them, *Komet* reached the Pacific via the North-East Passage, helped on her way by Soviet pilots and ice-breakers. Before she was sunk by the cruiser *Cornwall* on May 8, 1941, the *Pinguin* wrought havoc among Allied factory-ships and whale-catchers in the Antarctic. *Atlantis* was the most successful of them all. She passed the Denmark Strait at the beginning of April 1940, cruised right round the world, and on November 22, 1941, after 622 days at sea, was sunk in the South Atlantic by the cruiser *Devonshire*. The other four raiders all returned to western European ports and to Germany, as did some of their prizes.

Compared with the successes of the U-boats, the success of the German surface raiders in the second half of 1940 (62 ships sunk, and slightly less than 400,000 tons all told) appears somewhat modest. But their exploits had important strategic results. The British Admiralty made the decision to give battleship support to the convoys and from then on two or three battleships of the Home Fleet were always tied down on convoy escort duties.

On June 11, 1940, the first Italian submarine left La Spezia for the Atlantic and passed through the Strait of Gibraltar without trouble. It was eventually followed by 26 others, which the signing of the French armistice permitted to be based on Bordeaux. Thus was set up the *Comando Sommergibili Atlantici* or *Betasom*, under the command of Admiral Parona.

Unlike the German U-boats, the Italian submarines were much older both in design and construction. They lent themselves only badly to the "wolf-pack" tactics practised with such success by Dönitz's ships. Less manoeuvrable than their German opposite numbers, they suffered much more heavily in the storms of the North Atlantic.

The Italian submarines therefore tended to operate singly in more clement latitudes. But because the principal convoy routes led across the North Atlantic, the Italian contribution to the campaign against the Allied sealanes was modest.

CHAPTER 30
Help for Mussolini

By mid-December 1940 Germany could no longer ignore the successive land and sea defeats inflicted on the Italian forces in 1940 in Albania, at Taranto, and in Libya. If the grave consequences of the military crisis precipitated by Mussolini were not eliminated promptly and efficiently, the Germans feared that a political crisis would also ensue, and bring about the downfall of the only man in Italy who had Hitler's confidence.

The disturbing after-effects of the Duce's defeats were already apparent. On November 11 a parade of students, all carrying symbolical rods, had marched down the Champs-Elysées in Paris under the gaze of a sympathetic crowd. A little later, at Menton on the Franco-Italian frontier, placards appeared with the message; "This is French territory; Greeks, don't pursue the Italians past this point." But the most alarming incident took place at Vichy on December 13, when Pierre Laval was ousted from power by military force. Now there was considerable apprehension in German circles that General Weygand would throw in his lot with the Allies: he had already been appointed Delegate General of the French Government in French North Africa on October 3, with authority over Algeria, Tunisia, Morocco, and Senegal.

Hitler's plan for Spain

Hitler had no intention of being taken unawares. On December 10 he signed his Directive No. 19, which ordered Brauchitsch, Raeder, and Göring to take all necessary steps for the annexation of Unoccupied France. For this purpose, one column was to march from the region of Dijon down the valleys of the Saône and the Rhône, occupy Marseilles and then move towards Béziers, where it would join up with a column coming from Bordeaux via Toulouse and Narbonne. Two Panzer and four motorised divisions would take part in this operation, which was given the appropriate code-name "Attila". In addition, the Luftwaffe and German Navy were ordered to prevent the French fleet from leaving Toulon.

But it was doubtful whether the annexation of the Unoccupied Zone would have made up for the reappearance of North Africa as a factor in the war. If a new Franco-British front had been formed between Alexandria and Agadir, Italy's position, already critical, would have become almost desperate.

But meanwhile, in Albania, the Italians could rely on the bad weather of the winter and the rough conditions in the mountains to halt the impetus of the Greek counter-offensive. In the spring the Germans could therefore launch Operation "Marita", which would employ the German 12th Army (Field-Marshal List) and *Panzergruppe* Kleist, totalling five corps, made up of four Panzer divisions, one motorised division, two mountain divisions, and ten infantry divisions. In Libya, on the other hand, the débâcle at Sidi Barrani stressed the need for immediate action.

For this reason the Luftwaffe's X *Fliegerkorps* was sent south to bases in Sicily at the end of December 1940. Apart from its reconnaissance and fighter formations it consisted of two *Gruppen* of Junkers Ju 87 dive-bombers and two *Gruppen* of Ju 88 twin-engined bombers. The X *Fliegerkorps*

△ One of the many thousands of disillusioned Italian prisoners taken by the British XIII Corps during its beautifully timed advance to Beda Fomm and El Agheila. ▽ Mussolini's new "Roman Empire" crumbles around him as the "Wolves of Tuscany" cur slinks away with its tail between its legs: a cartoon by David Low.

was under the command of Luftwaffe General Geissler, who had harrassed Allied shipping in Norwegian waters earlier in the year; its mission now was to close the Mediterranean to the British between Sicily and Tunisia and to engage in combat the British aircraft based on Malta. On January 10, 1941, X *Fliegerkorps* opened its account by launching heavy attacks against the British aircraft-carrier *Illustrious*.

On the 11th, Hitler issued 13 copies of his Directive No. 22: "German support for battles in the Mediterranean area". The introduction was worded as follows: "The

△ *A sentry stands guard over one of the rainwater catchment slopes on the Rock of Gibraltar. Though a good defensive position, Gibraltar would be poorly placed to withstand a prolonged siege if Spain entered the war. Hence the honeycomb of galleries driven through the rock as magazines, store-rooms, barracks, and enormous reservoirs.*

situation in the Mediterranean area, where England is employing superior forces against our allies, requires that Germany should assist for reasons of strategy, politics, and psychology.

"Tripolitania must be held and the danger of a collapse on the Albanian front must be eliminated. Furthermore the Cavallero Army Group [in Albania] must be enabled, in co-operation with the later operations of 12th Army, to go over to the offensive from Albania."

Hitler therefore ordered O.K.H. to form "a special detachment [*Sperrverband*] sufficient to render valuable service to our allies in the defence of Tripolitania,

particularly against British armoured divisions."

The preparations for the intervention of a German mountain division in Albania came to nothing: Mussolini actually declined its services. However, Operation *Sonnenblume* ("Sunflower"), which led to the creation of the Afrika Korps, went ahead.

It was intended to engage a German force in the defence of Tripoli, not to launch it on a campaign to conquer Egypt and seize the Suez Canal. The decision was taken because the German High Command curiously overestimated the strength of the British. The Germans took the assessment of their allies at face value: in fact, the Italians believed that Wavell had 17 full strength divisions, with another four in the process of embarking in Britain, and at least 1,100 aircraft.

Objective Gibraltar

Meanwhile, the German plans to seize the Rock of Gibraltar for the Axis were nearing completion. Field-Marshal von Reichenau was to command the operation, which was code-named "Felix". He had under his command two Panzer divisions, three motorised divisions, and a mountain division, supported by the Luftwaffe's VIII *Fliegerkorps*–eight Stuka *Gruppen*, two fighter *Gruppen*, and five reconnaissance squadrons. The question of Portugal remained to be settled; if, contrary to Hitler's expectations, President Salazar appealed to Britain, Reichenau's forces would leave their planned route (Irun-Burgos-Seville) at Cáceres and head for Lisbon along the left bank of the Tagus.

The assault on Gibraltar was to be entrusted to the XLIX *Gebirgskorps* (General Kübler). According to the calculations of General Brand, head of artillery at O.K.H., the fortress had 154 guns, including 56 A.A. guns; and the neck of land connecting the Rock to the mainland was exposed to the fire of 1 guns in concrete casemates. General Kübler was therefore to be given about 50 heavy batteries with 8,500 tons of ammunition to strengthen his normal quota of artillery. In addition the Germans were planning to use hitherto untried weapon for this operation, including "*Mörse Karl*": a self-propelled tracked vehicl with a 60-cm (23½-inch) mortar, which fired a 2.2-ton armour-piercing shell over a range of about 4½ miles. This huge 132-ton vehicle was powered by a 580-hp engine, and therefore had a certain mobility. Moreover, in his diary Halder several times mentions a plan to cause explosions in the Rock's galleries.

Supported by this powerful artillery force and by General von Richthofen's Stukas, General Hubert Lanz's division would launch the final attack on the fortress. On the right the *Grossdeutschland* motorised regiment would take the port of Gibraltar with the help of assault-boats; on the left the 98th *Gebirgsjäger*

Admiral Canaris, head of the *Abwehr*, was instructed to go to Madrid at the end of December 1940 to explain Hitler's intention to Franco and to ask him to open the Spanish frontier on January 10; Reichenau would then be able to launch the attack on Gibraltar on February 8. Once again, however, Franco fell back on his previously-stated conditions; and on February 12 Mussolini, who had been charged by Hitler with the task of getting Franco to declare himself openly, was also unsuccessful in his mission when he met the Caudillo at Bordighera in Italy.

Regiment (mountain troops) would capture the Rock, whose summit towers 1,400 feet above sea level.

The Strait blocked

Operation "Felix" would be completed when coastal batteries (15-cm and 24-cm) had been established at Ceuta and Tarifa, commanding the strait, while a Panzer division and a motorised division were sent into Spanish Morocco. Weygand and Pétain, it was confidently believed, would be powerless to intervene.

· LIDDELL UNION ·

FORDHAM'S FLATS
CALPE SHELTER
WILLIS ELBOW
WILLIS ROAD
WATERWORKS TUNNEL

The Italian Carro Armato M11/39 medium tank

Weight: 10.8 tons.
Crew: 3.
Armament: one 37-mm gun with 84 rounds and two 8-mm Breda M38 machine guns with 2,800 rounds.
Armour: hull nose, driver's plate, and turret front 30-mm; glacis plate, hull sides, and turret sides and rear 14-mm; hull belly 10-mm; hull decking 8-mm; turret roof 7-mm; and engine covers 6-mm.
Engine: FIAT SPA 8T diesel, 105-hp.
Speed: 20.5 mph maximum (on roads).
Range: 124 miles.
Length: 15 feet 6½ inches.
Width: 7 feet 1½ inches.
Height: 7 feet 4½ inches.

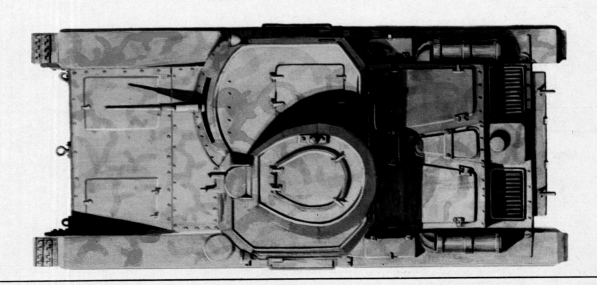

Mussolini's strange behaviour

It should be stressed that Mussolini pleaded Hitler's case extremely gently. He told Franco what he had said to Hitler: "I'll talk, but I won't exert any pressure"; and this was hardly likely to persuade Franco to take the decisive step. Moreover, Mussolini seemed to be offering a loop-hole which Franco was quick to take. According to the official Italian record of the meeting, Mussolini stated:

"The Duce reminds the Caudillo that he had always shown great discretion and consideration for the attitude of Spain. [This was a veiled criticism of Hitler.] He agrees with the Caudillo's view that Spain cannot remain neutral, but he believes that the timing and manner of Spain's entry into the war is entirely her own affair. Participation in war is too serious a matter for it to be precipitated by outside influences."

To explain Mussolini's strange behaviour one can only hazard a few guesses. It seems safe to assume that he did not want Operation "Felix" to be successful. If Gibraltar fell, Germany would replace Britain as the master of the western entrance to the Mediterranean; and Mussolini had laid down the neutralisation of the Strait of Gibraltar as one of Fascist Italy's war aims.

Hitler received an Italian memorandum giving the rather negative results of the interview, and on February 28 he noted Franco's evasion, which showed the classic skill of a bullfighter. Resentfully, Hitler stated to Mussolini:

"In any case the outcome of the Spaniards' lengthy chattering and their written explanations is that Spain doesn't want to go to war and will not do so. This is extremely irksome because for the moment the opportunity to strike England in the simplest manner possible, in her Mediterranean possessions, is lost."

This may well have been the case, but clearly the continued run of Italian defeats in Libya encouraged Franco to go on waiting.

The Italians did make some half-hearted attempts to put pressure on Spain to take an active part in Operation "Felix". An example is the following passage from a letter from Ciano to Suñer on June 3, 1941 – particularly the curious postscript in which Mussolini left Franco an easy way out:

"My dear Ramon,

I am writing to you on my return from the meeting at the Brenner. I am sure you will be pleased to hear that both we and the Germans discussed Spanish matters with great interest, and that the Axis powers regard their friendship with your country as a matter of vital importance.

"The events of recent weeks are of great significance in the conduct of the war. The Balkans have now been cleared of British influence. The British Navy has lost many of its bases and is being caught in an increasingly closing vice by the Axis

forces. A day will come – it's not far off – when the Mediterranean will be free of the presence of the British fleet. Can Nationalist, Falangist Spain remain indifferent and neutral in the face of these events which have such great significance for our lives and for the future of the Mediterranean countries? As a sincere and well-tried friend of Spain, I don't think so." A further plea by Ciano follows, and then the Duce's final, modest entreaty: "Spain must *at least* join the Tripartite Pact, and before other countries do so at that. In subscribing to the Tripartite Pact, Spain will be in a position to influence the future settlement of Europe."

△ *Architects of desert victory: General Sir Archibald Wavell, General Officer Commanding-in-Chief, Middle East and, on the left, Lieutenant-General Sir Richard O'Connor, commander of XIII Corps.*

The British invade Libya

On January 10, 1941, the British Western Desert Force was designated XIII Corps with its commander, Lieutenant-General O'Connor, directly responsible to G.H.Q. Cairo. This simplified the chain of command as the middle echelon, the "Army of the Nile", was abolished; in any event the latter had been pure fiction, a paper army intended to impress the Italians. Lieutenant-General Maitland Wilson, commander of the "Army of the Nile", was seconded to other duties.

On the 1st, XIII Corps was preparing to attack the fortress of Bardia, which was protected by a fortified perimeter 18 miles long. Small forts had been built at a distance of about 800 yards from each other along this perimeter, which consisted of an anti-tank ditch 13 feet wide and about 4 feet deep, behind which was a barbed-wire network and minefields. Behind this perimeter, which had been carefully strengthened along its southern face, was another defensive position.

Lieutenant-General Annibale Bergonzoli, commander of the Italian XXIII Corps, had been entrusted with the defence of Bardia in an urgent telegram from Mussolini. For this purpose he had the "Marmarica" Division (General Tracchia), the "23rd of March" Division (General Antonelli), some Fascist militia, plus survivors from the "Catanzaro" and "Cirene" Divisions.

General O'Connor had no chance of opening his attack with tanks, as he had done at Sidi Barrani, as the tank battalion supporting his infantry had only 23 tanks left (as a result of the lack of spare parts) out of the 57 which he had had on December 8. The infantry of the 6th Australian Division would therefore have to cross the anti-tank ditch, using a specially-built assault bridge, and clear the mines with the help of the sappers, to allow the remaining Matildas to exploit the breach thus made in the Italian defences.

The attack was launched at the western sector of the perimeter, which was not as strongly defended as the southern face. At 0530 hours on January 3 the Australians went into the anti-tank ditch; an hour later they had cleared two mine-free passages, and the tanks went through them towards Bardia town, which had been bombarded by the Royal Navy and the R.A.F. On the next day the victors reached the sea, having cut the Italian garrison in two. The Italians capitulated on January 5, surrendering to XIII Corps 45,000 prisoners, 460 guns, 131 (mainly light) tanks, and over 700 trucks.

Greece or Libya?

At this point the question of British intervention in Greece was raised again. On November 2, 1940, during his visit to Cairo, Anthony Eden had received a message from Churchill asking him to reinforce General Papagos's air force at the expense of the Middle East theatre. Eden had irreverently scribbled over the despatch: "Egypt more important than Greece. Enemy air power in Libya unaltered."

After this the problem of British intervention had been shelved, as the Italians suffered successive defeats in Epirus and Albania. It was discussed again, however, when news reached London about the German concentrations in Rumania, and there was much speculation as to their possible objectives. Eden, who had just

exchanged the War Ministry for the Foreign Office, found himself compelled to reverse his views on the relative importance of Greece and Egypt.

In Churchill's view, after the fall of Bardia, aid to Greece became more important than the operations in Libya, which were to be halted at Tobruk.

O'Connor takes Tobruk

The capture of this deep-water port, built in a well-protected bay, would offer the British forces in Libya the opportunity of using the sea route for replenishing their supplies rather than relying on the 375 mile overland route between Alexandria and Tobruk. A single 6,000 ton merchantman can carry a cargo equivalent to the load of 600 to 1,200 trucks, each with a driver and his mate; this makes for a considerable saving in fuel as well as manpower. Moreover, the Tobruk fortress included El Adem, an important airfield which British aircraft could use as a forward base. The Tobruk defences were similar to those of Bardia, but they were still partly under construction and had a perimeter of about

△ ◁ Dawn, January 3, 1941: Australian infantry move up towards Bardia. In the subsequent attack they took 8,000 Italian prisoners (top). Men of the 6th Australian Division advance behind a Matilda tank (bottom).
▽ "The Battle of Egypt. Italian Prisoners" by Anthony Gross. The scruffy listlessness of most such prisoners is particularly well caught.

▷ *After breaking through the Italians' perimeter defences around Bardia and seizing a bridgehead across the anti-tank ditch, infantry wait for bridging equipment and the arrival of the tanks before pushing on towards Bardia itself.*
▽ *British artillery, ready to support the infantry assaulting Tobruk on January 21.*

40 miles. The garrison, under Genera Pitassi Mannella, commander of the Ital an XXII Corps, consisted mainly of th "Sirte" Division (General Della Mura).

Without waiting for the fall of Bardi O'Connor had sent the 7th Armoure Division to cut Tobruk's communication After the 6th Australian Division ha joined up with 7th Armoured, O'Conno started the attack on Tobruk at dawn o January 21. As he only had 12 Matild tanks left, he supplemented them b mechanising a squadron of Australia cavalry, giving them some Italian M-13/4 tanks.

General Pitassi Mannella was appa ently surprised by the speed with whic O'Connor had prepared this new manoe vre. In spite of a few energetic counte attacks everything was over by nightfa as the Italian artillery had been put out action by the British armour. By th following afternoon O'Connor had adde 25,000 prisoners, 208 guns, 23 mediu tanks, and 200 trucks to his bag. He ha advanced so rapidly that the sea-wate distilling plant fell intact into the hand of the British, and the Tobruk port in stallations were working again in a fe days. The 6th Australian Division lost 17 dead and 638 wounded in the attacks o Bardia and Tobruk, which were ene getically conducted at all levels.

The British were firmly settled i Mussolini's North African empire.

The Italian Autoblinda 40 armoured car

Weight: $7\frac{1}{2}$ tons.
Crew: four.
Armament: three 8-mm Breda M38 machine guns.
Engine: SPA 6-cylinder, 80-hp.
Speed: 47 mph.
Range: 250 miles.
Length: 17 feet 2 inches.
Width: 6 feet 4 inches.
Height: 8 feet.

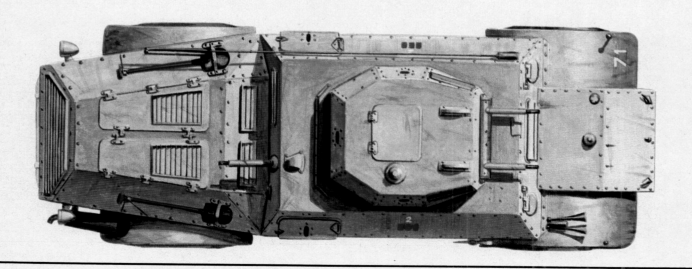

△ △ *A short rest for British infantry before starting the final advance on Tobruk. In the background can be seen the smoke of burning supply dumps.*
△ *Italian shipping sunk in Tobruk harbour. What they could not get away, the Italians tried to destroy, but the speed of the British and Australian victory meant that much of value to the occupiers survived.*

Greece gets top priority

After the capture of Tobruk, the question for the British was whether or not to go for Benghazi. Churchill did not exclude this possibility in the appreciation he drew up for the Chiefs-of-Staff Committee on January 6, 1941, but he regarded it as of secondary importance to supporting the Greeks and helping them to take Valona. In Section 13 of this lengthy document he wrote: "It would not be right for the sake of Benghazi to lose the chance of the Greeks taking Valona, and thus to dispirit or anger them, and perhaps make them in the mood for a separate peace with Italy. Therefore the prospect must be faced that after Tobruk the further west-ward advance of the Army of the Nile may be seriously cramped. It is quite clear to me that supporting Greece must have priority after the western flank of Egypt has been made secure."

But by January 10 Valona was no longer the key objective. The German concentration in Rumania could no longer be interpreted as a manoeuvre in a war of nerves: it was clearly the first stage of a large-scale military campaign, and Greece seemed to be the inevitable objective. Faced with the threat of a new disaster in the Balkans, British military aid to the Greek Army became a matter of vital importance. Churchill therefore sent new instructions to General Wavell, from which we may quote an extract:

"You must now therefore conform your plans to larger interests at stake.
"3. Nothing must hamper capture of Tobruk, but thereafter all operations in Libya are subordinated to aiding Greece, and all preparations must be made from the receipt of this telegram for the immediate succour of Greece . . .
"4. We expect and require prompt and active compliance with our decisions, for which we bear full responsibility."

The Chiefs-of-Staffs Committee endorsed the text of this telegram, which revealed certain differences of opinion between London and G.H.Q. Cairo. But when the Greek Government declined to accept British aid under the terms offered, agreement between the two headquarters was restored for the time being.

General Wavell and Air Chief-Marshal

Longmore flew to Athens on January 14 and conferred with General Metaxas, King George II of the Hellenes, and General Papagos on the subject of British aid.

According to Metaxas, if Germany should invade Bulgarian territory, neither Yugoslavia nor Turkey would abandon their neutrality unless it were first violated by the Germans. Papagos then described the current military situation within this diplomatic and political context, and gave his own appreciation of the situation for the benefit of the two British commanders.

Twelve Greek divisions, three infantry brigades, and a cavalry division were holding the Albanian front. The 6th, 7th, 12th, and 14th Divisions were facing the Bulgarian frontier but the 6th was about to leave for the western Macedonian sector, as the Italians were increasing their strength there every day.

From all the information at the disposal of the Greeks, it appeared that the Germans had at least 12 divisions–including two or three Panzer divisions–in Rumania; in Bulgaria, under the direction of German officers in civilian clothes, the airfields were being improved, some new ones were being built, and the roads leading to the frontier were being repaired. It was clear from these preparations that in all probability the main force of the German or German-Bulgarian offensive would be aimed at eastern Macedonia, with Salonika as its main objective.

"I therefore concluded," states Papagos in his book *Greece at War*, "that in the present political and military situation, in order to have a stable defensive front the Greek armies would have to be reinforced as soon as possible by nine divisions and the appropriate aircraft from Great Britain." In addition, the Allies would have to act quickly to man the western Thracian and eastern Macedonian sectors before the German forces in Rumania had taken up their offensive dispositions along the Bulgarian-Greek frontier. Papagos also suggested a series of both logistic and defensive (anti-aircraft) measures which would, in his opinion, speed up operations and make up for the advantage gained by the Germans.

All this makes it hard to agree with Churchill's statement that in these meetings, of which Major-General Heywood and Colonel Kitrilakis drew up the official record, "the Greek government were unwilling that any of our troops should land in Salonika until they would do so in sufficient numbers to act offensively."

Whatever may have been the origin of this obvious misunderstanding, Wavell emphasised to his allies that the only forces he could afford to dispatch immediately to the Greek theatre of operations consisted of an artillery regiment, a mixed A.A. and anti-tank regiment, and an armoured group with about 60 armoured cars. Britain, he added, could certainly send two or three divisions with an air formation to follow this first contingent; but as he had no shipping immediately available, he would need two or three months to transport this second detachment to the scene of operations.

Generals Metaxas and Papagos were very much taken aback by the British proposals. The immediate dispatch to Greece of 24 field guns, 12 heavy howitzers, 24 anti-tank guns, 40 A.A. guns, and 65 light and medium tanks would not add to the defensive power of the Greek Army in any way, although it would give Hitler an excuse to bring forward his plans.

Wavell's second proposal, however, while still unsatisfactory, was better than nothing; they therefore accepted it, although they did not think that it matched the menace of the German presence in Bulgaria. A note containing these views was sent to the British Ambassador on January 18, 1941. Confirming the attitude of General Papagos, Metaxas noted in his preamble: "We are resolved to resist the German attack, if it is made, by every means and at any price; but we have no wish to provoke it in any way, unless the aid which Great Britain can lend us in Macedonia is sufficient for this purpose."

▽ *A group of Italian prisoners, caught trying to escape to Tobruk from Bardia, waits on the quayside at Sollum to embark on the ship that will carry them to captivity in Egypt.*

THE LONDON BLITZ

Shortly after we'd gone to bed there was a violent explosion as a thousand-pound bomb landed about a quarter of a mile away. Mereworth, a substantial eighteenth century house, shook violently. A moment later we were out in the corridor asking each other what had happened. The old gentleman was missing. We went into his room and found him sitting up in bed reading, with the windows open and the lights blazing. We snapped them off, admonishing him indignantly, then went downstairs and walked onto the terrace. We could hear guns in the distance and the pink glow seemed to be growing brighter. We went into the drawing-room and turned on the radio, hoping to hear some news, but all we got was a series of Hawaiian melodies from America. Anne cheered everyone up by saying that the dome on top of the house probably looked like a huge gasometer from the air and would certainly be taken for a military objective.

The next morning we learned that London was still standing. Miles of East End houses had been destroyed however, and thousands of people were homeless. I was returning in the afternoon and had arranged to have tea with a friend in Brentwood on the way. To get there, I had to drive to Gravesend, about fifteen miles away, and ferry

across the Thames; although it seemed doubtful that the roads would be passable, I started off about three o'clock in the afternoon.

The countryside had such a complacent look about it, it was hard to believe that anything out of the ordinary had happened. The first I saw was when I reached the ferry: great clouds of dark smoke were pouring down the estuary from the Woolwich docks. No one seemed disconcerted, however, for the Sunday afternoon scene was as peaceful as ever: the two ferrymen basking lazily in the sun; one of the dock-workers reading the morning paper; and the ticket-collector grumbling that the Huns were a noisy lot and he hadn't had a wink of sleep. From his bored tone of voice, you might have thought the disturbance had been caused by nothing more unusual than a cat on the back fence.

From Tilbury to Brentwood, another fifteen miles, I passed about a half a dozen smashed buildings, and made several diversions where time-bombs had fallen; but on the whole the area seemed surprisingly free of damage. When I arrived at the hotel I found my friend, an officer in an artillery regiment, in high spirits. I commented on the burning warehouses, but he waved my remarks aside, insisting that the Germans' primary aim was not

the docks but to spread alarm and despondency by knocking out all the saloons and pubs. The bombers had come over again that afternoon, but the British fighters still had their tails up. He had just come from an aerodrome where a fighter squadron was operating, and said that many of the pilots were coming in doing the "victory roll". One fighter did three victory rolls and the ground workers cheered.

I left for London, about twenty miles away, at seven-thirty. If I had realized that the blitz of the night before was to be repeated, I would have taken care to get

1. *Heinkel 111's over London. The Luftwaffe had sowed the wind; would Germany now reap the whirlwind? The Germans thought not, as it was imagined that no-one could survive such a bombardment with their morale intact; the British had other ideas.* 2. *London in flames: a photograph taken from the dome of St. Paul's on the night of December 29, 1940.* 3. *A rescue squad brings out a man buried for 14 hours in the wreckage of his home. At first such tribulations merely strengthened the "Bulldog spirit". But things were to alter later.*

4. Girls of the Auxiliary Territorial Service manning the range finder and predictor on an anti-aircraft gun site. 5. The major targets in Britain, according to the February 1941 *Signal*. The red stars and diamonds mark naval bases of primary and secondary importance; looped black bars shipyards; anchors within circles ports; flags garrisons; red circles the centres of oil distribution; blue circles aircraft factories; green circles grain centres; black circles the steel and metal industry; brown areas coal mining; and two black bars iron ore. 6. Girls of the Women's Auxiliary Air Force at work on a barrage balloon in Central London. 7. The galleries of the Queen's Hall after a raid. 8. Londoners asleep on the escalators of an Underground station. 9. Damage to the House of Commons. 10. Westminster Abbey, looking towards the altar, after being bombed. 11. A scene typical of the "Blitz"–civilians sheltering in a tube station.

home before the sirens sounded. As it was, the mournful wail sounded a few minutes after I had started. It was getting dark and I drove as fast as possible to make the best of the light. Although I was travelling through one of the most congested London suburbs (Stratford—a mile or so from East Ham), the streets were clearing rapidly; people were running for shelter in all directions, and buses and trucks were coming to a stop. Lines of tramcars stood empty. Soon there was an ominous silence and mine was practically the only car on the road.

Two stranded soldiers waved to me and I stopped and gave them a lift. It was difficult driving in the semi-darkness and the quiet was oppressive. Suddenly, a few hundred yards ahead of us, we heard a sickening whistle and a deafening explosion. A bomb landed in the middle of the street and there was a shower of glass and débris from the houses on either side. The whistles blew and A.R.P. workers and special police deputies were on the job almost immediately; it was too dark to see what damage had been done to the houses, but the street was covered with rubble.

The police warned us to be careful and détoured us round to another road. Soon we heard an ambulance siren ringing. Ahead of us the sky had lit up in a red glow and we could hear more bombs dropping in the darkness. We closed all the windows in order not to be hit by flying shrapnel (the wrong thing to do) and continued on our way. The soldiers were quiet. It was so dark I couldn't see them very well; they were just shapes in the back of the car. Occasionally one of them muttered: "We'll get them for this," but that was all. Their destination was London Bridge and, somehow, with the sound of the bombs and the guns, and the sky a deep fire pink, I couldn't help thinking of the old nursery rhyme: "London Bridge is falling down." They evidently thought of it too, for I heard one of them saying to the other: "I'll lay you odds the old bridge isn't down," and he was right, for a mile or so later it loomed up in front of us as solid and substantial as ever.

I then drove through the heart of the City which seemed as eerie and deserted as a graveyard. I stopped to ask the way of an A.R.P. warden and he asked me to take two of his workers up to Piccadilly. The men hadn't had their clothes off for forty-eight hours. They had just come from a building where five people were dug out of the ruins. "Three women and two children," one of them told me grimly: then, almost under his breath: "The price is going to be high for the Germans when the war is over."

I finally reached Montagu Square and found Mr. and Mrs. Kinch (the caretaker and his wife) in the kitchen, calmly having their supper. Overhead you could hear the sound of the planes, and every now and then the house shook and the windows rattled as a bomb dropped somewhere in the vicinity. I asked them if they weren't afraid and Mrs. Kinch said: "Oh, no. If we were, what good would it do us?"

The next morning the sky was blue and innocent. If you hadn't seen the yawning craters and the wreckage, you might have thought that you dreamt it. Traffic was normal, the shops were full, old ladies sunned themselves in the park, and soldiers and their girl friends strolled down Piccadilly arm in arm. I lunched at the Berkeley restaurant and found it as noisy and crowded as ever. Suddenly there was a bang. The room shook as a time-bomb exploded a few blocks away. A pretty girl in a saucy hat turned to the young army subaltern with her, and said, in a voice that rang across the restaurant: "Did you drop something?"

[From Looking for Trouble, by Virginia Cowles, published by Hamish Hamilton.]

12. *Cannon Street viewed from the Stone Gallery of St. Paul's* 13. *The same view after the fire raid of December 29, 1940 and subsequent bombing in the next four months. The first street on the right is Old Change. Next is Distaff Lane (opposite which used to be Cordwainers' Hall). The third and fourth turnings on the right are Friday Street and Bread Street. The church in the left background is Sir Christopher Wren's church of St. Mary Aldermary. In the right background are visible the gutted roof of Cannon Street Station with Tower Bridge behind.* 14. *A poster urges shoppers to avoid the rush hours and thus allow the transport system to run more efficiently and consequently more economically.* 15. *Britain's latest imports, according to the* Lustige Blätter *of Berlin: Churchill, with the luxury of brandy and cigars to hand, has a German bomb rammed down his throat in the ruins of London.* 16. *Although barrage balloons did not take a great toll of the German bombers, they did force them to fly higher, where the accuracy of their bomb aiming was impaired.* 17. *Bomb damage in London's Temple area.* 18. *Soldiers carefully prop up an unexploded German bomb before the disposal team arrives.*

CHAPTER 31
Tripoli in danger

△ *Italian prisoners taken at Tobruk march towards a temporary prison camp.*

▷▷ *The team that won Britain's first victories of the war: infantry and tanks. In the desert, the mixed force of British, Australian, New Zealand, and Indian infantry was much more than a match for the Italians, and the tanks, though few in number, were either too fast and enterprising (as were the Vickers Mark VI) or heavily armoured (the Matilda) for the totally inadequate Italian armoured forces.*

After receiving this reassuring confirmation of Greece's intentions, the British Government made no attempt to influence the Greek Government. On January 21, the very day of the attack on Tobruk, London, now free from any urgent Greek commitments, ordered G.H.Q. Cairo to resume its offensive towards Benghazi without further delay.

After the surprise attack on Sidi Barrani, Marshal Graziani had given his opinion that Cyrenaica could no longer be defended and that it would be advisable to withdraw to Tripoli, putting the Sirte Desert between his 10th Army and the Army of the Nile. When the Italian High Command recommended him to be more optimistic, Graziani set to work to improvise the defence of Cyrenaica—but it must be admitted that he did not make a very good job of it. His 10th Army was divided into three defensive groups: XXIII Corps at Bardia, XXII Corps at Tobruk, and the XX Corps (General Cona) holding the Mechili-Derna line. This disposition meant that it was highly likely that 10th Army could be defeated piece-meal by an enemy who was greatly inferior in overall numbers.

On January 9, despite the destruction of XXIII Corps in the battle for Bardia, Graziani was now showing optimism instead of his previous pessimism. In fact the Jebel Akhdar, the massif between Mechili and Derna which rises to a height of about 1,650 feet, was quite unsuitable for an attack by mechanised forces.

By putting an infantry division into the Derna position and the armoured brigade of General Babini into Mechili, Graziani thought he would have an excellent chance of halting the British advance towards Benghazi. But he was forgetting that those two formations would have to fight independently as they were separated by the Jebel Akhdar hills and could not reinforce one another.

On January 24 the 6th Australian Division approached the Derna position, while the 7th Armoured Division fell upon Babini's armoured brigade, in spite of the extremely poor state of the British tanks. The Italian 14-ton tanks were fighting the same number of 12.5-ton British cruiser tanks, and the battle ended badly for the Italians. They retreated into the Jebel Akhdar to avoid encirclement—but in so doing they gave the British a clear road to the main Italian supply-line along the Gulf of Sirte. For this reason Graziani decided to abandon western Cyrenaica on February 1. General Gariboldi was sent to Tripoli to organise the defence of the province, and General Tellera succeeded him as commander of 10th Army.

The distance between Mechili and Beda Fomm, near the Gulf of Sirte, is about 140 miles. Along the coast road between Derna and Beda Fomm the distance is about 225 miles. But the retreating Italians had the advantage of using the *Via Balbia*, the excellent coast road; the British, advancing from Mechili towards Beda Fomm, had only a poorly reconnoitred track, which was not clearly marked and which crossed a desert consisting either of soft sand or of areas strewn with large rocks.

"War is won with leftovers", Marshal Foch had once said. It is hardly likely that Generals O'Connor and O'Moore Creagh, commander of 7th Armoured Division, had ever heard of this dictum, but now they put it into practice with a vengeance. At 1500 hours on February 4 the 11th Hussars (Colonel Combe) were at Msus, only 60 miles from the *Via Balbia*. At

dawn on the 5th, after they had been reinforced with some artillery, they took the track leading to Antelat and at noon reached their objective at Beda Fomm, half an hour before the first Italian column retreating from Benghazi down the *Via Balbia*. Confused engagements were fought throughout February 6, with the Italians hitting out wildly as they came up against the British blocking their retreat.

Finally, at 0900 hours of February 7, O'Connor sent an uncoded signal for the information of Wavell and the edification of Mussolini: "Fox killed in the open." Badly wounded, General Tellera died a few hours later; the H.Q. of 10th Army, and Generals Cona and Babini, had been captured. General Bergonzoli had also been captured: he had managed to make his way through the Australian lines when Bardia fell. About 20,000 Italians were also captured, and the final count of the equipment seized by the British after this last battle amounted to 112 11- and 14-ton M 11 and 13 medium tanks, 216 guns, and 1,500 vehicles.

On February 3 the British had reached El Agheila at the bottom of the Gulf of Sirte. This was a very important position, for there was only a narrow gap about 15-20 miles wide through which tanks could pass between the desert and the sea.

▲ *Marshal Graziani, relieved of his command on February 10.*

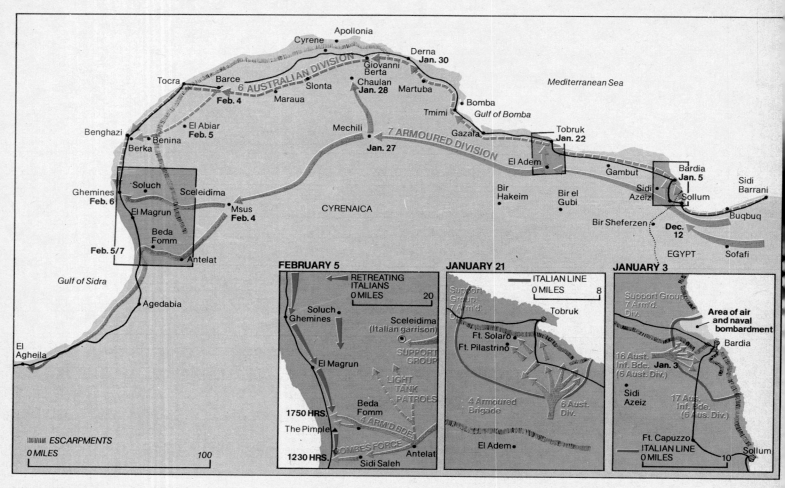

As the British XIII Corps now commanded this position, it was well placed to invade Tripolitania or defend Cyrenaica as required.

Wavell's original five-day raid had developed into a two-month campaign. In four pitched battles O'Connor had advanced 560 miles from his starting position. Although he never had more than two divisions under his command, he had destroyed one Italian army (four corps, or nine divisions) at a cost of only 500 dead, 1,373 wounded, and 56 missing. The "bag" of Italian prisoners amounted to 130,000 men, including 22 generals and one admiral, and O'Connor had seized or destroyed 845 guns and 380 tanks. For the third time in the war Guderian's words to Hitler had been proved true: "Tanks are a life-saving weapon".

Graziani steps down

On February 10 Marshal Graziani was ordered to hand over his command to General Gariboldi and to return to Italy. His conduct of operations was carefully examined by a commission of enquiry, which came to highly equivocal conclusions about them. But it was hard to assign him the total responsibility for this catastrophe without implicating the Duce himself. Undoubtedly, Graziani had not excelled himself; possibly, also, he still suffered from the effects of the hand-grenade which had been thrown at him in Addis Ababa in 1938. But above all he had been hampered by his shortage of modern weapons, just as had Gamelin in the French campaign a few months earlier.

On December 27, after the battle of Sidi Barrani, Graziani had attempted to explain matters to Mussolini. "From the harsh experience of these bitter days," he wrote, "we must conclude that in this theatre of war a single armoured division is more powerful than a whole army."

Coming events would prove these to be prophetic words.

The Luftwaffe strikes

The Wehrmacht's intervention in the Mediterreanean theatre began when the German High Command transferred X *Fliegerkorps* to Sicily and Calabria.

Admiral Sir Andrew Cunningham was born in 1883. In 1939 he was C.-in-C., Mediterranean, and when Italy entered the war he soon found himself outnumbered and in difficult straits strategically and logistically. He quickly wrested command from the Italians, however, in several actions at sea and at Taranto, and thus secured the army's right flank. Cunningham became Allied Naval C.-in-C. under Eisenhower in 1943, and First Sea Lord in October of the same year.

At the end of December 1940, General Geissler of the Luftwaffe set up his H.Q. at Taormina. His squadrons were divided between the airfields at Catania, Comiso, Marsala, Trápani, Palermo, and Reggio di Calabria, along with 45 Italian bombers and 75 Italian fighters. Together with the 70 bombers and 25 fighters of the *Regia Aeronautica* based in Sardinia, the number of Axis aircraft capable of operating in the central Mediterranean, which narrows to under 90 miles between Cape Bon in Tunisia and Marsala in Sicily, was approximately 400.

Such a force should normally have been under the command of *Superaero*, the High Command of the Italian Air Force. But Göring had no intention of permitting this, for he deliberately kept "his" airmen under his own control and reserved to himself the right to give them orders. Thus it is fairly certain that he was responsible for continual interference and fraction in the conduct of operations.

The strength of the R.A.F. on Malta was far smaller. When X *Fliegerkorps* moved south, the British air defences of Malta consisted of a dozen Swordfish, 16 Hurricanes, 16 Wellington twin-engine bombers, and a few Martin Maryland bomber/reconnaissance aircraft built in the United States. Admittedly a new shipload of 16 Hurricanes was expected with the next convoy from Gibraltar, but this was still a drop in the ocean.

General Geissler and his aircrews got their first chance to distinguish themselves with the British Operation "Excess", which started on January 6. Admiral Somerville's task was to convoy four merchantmen (one for Malta, the others for Greece) from Gibraltar to the central Mediterranean. Admiral Cunningham in Alexandria would make use of the appearance of Force H in the Western Mediterranean to send two merchantment into Malta. At the same time,

two cruisers from his light forces would take troops there. After that he would take charge of the ships making for Greece from Gibraltar.

While the two British convoys converged on Malta from east and west, the Malta-based bombers struck at Naples on the night of January 8–9. Their target was the Italian battleships which had survived the Taranto raid. The *Giulio Cesare* suffered a leak as the result of a bomb explosion on the bottom of the harbour and had to steam to Genoa for repairs. The *Vittorio Veneto* escaped untouched, but *Supermarina* decided to transfer her to La Spezia, where she would be out of range of the Malta-based bombers. This, however, would prevent *Vittorio Veneto* from taking any useful action in the narrows between Tunisia and Sicily.

Force H completed its mission without incident. Somerville passed to the south of Sardinia on the evening of January 9 and returned to Gibraltar with the battleship *Malaya*, the battle-cruiser *Renown*, and the aircraft-carrier *Ark Royal*, leaving his charges under the protection of an A.A. cruiser, two heavy cruisers (*Gloucester* and *Southampton*, which had joined him after landing the troops they had

△ ◁ *The advance from Sidi Barrani to El Agheila.* ▽ *Two British soldiers inspect the gutted wreckage of a FIAT C.R. 42 fighter. This, the best such aircraft available to the Italians in North Africa, was no match for the Hurricanes of the R.A.F. and about equal to the Gladiator.* ▽ ▽ *Australian artillery in action before Derna, which was evacuated by the Italians on January 30.*

△ *"Italian bombers over Malta",
the somewhat fanciful title to
an equally optimistic painting
in* Signal. *The truth is, to say
the least of things, different:
despite the enormous numerical
superiority over the R.A.F.
enjoyed by the* Regia
Aeronautica, *the defence of the
island was not hard pressed until
the advent of the German X
Fliegerkorps at its bases in Sicily.*
▷ ▷ *Italian cruisers on convoy
escort duties in the
Mediterranean. On the whole,
however, the use of such forces
was unambitious in the extreme,
even allowing for the fact that oil
fuel was in short supply and
there was no air cover worthy
of the name.*

brought from Alexandria in Malta), and
five destroyers. At dawn on January 10
the *Gloucester* and *Southampton* sank the
Italian torpedo-boat *Vega* which had tried
heroically to attack them. During this
action, the destroyer *Gallant* hit a mine
and had to be towed to Malta. Repairs
proved impossible, however, because of
Axis air attacks.

Ordeal of the *Illustrious*

But Cunningham's Mediterranean Fleet
did not get off so easily. Towards 1230
hours Junkers Ju 87 and Ju 88 bombers
appeared over the British fleet, which had
joined the convoy soon after the sinking
of the *Vega*, and launched a fierce attack

on the aircraft-carrier *Illustrious*, in spite
of sustained fire from the battleships
Warspite and *Valiant*.

"There was no doubt we were watching
complete experts," wrote Admiral Cunningham in his memoirs. "Formed rough-
ly in a larger circle over the fleet they
peeled off one by one when reaching the
attacking position. We could not but
admire the skill and precision of it all.
The attacks were pressed home to point-
blank range, and as they pulled out of
their dives some of them were seen to fly
along the flight deck of the *Illustrious*
below the level of her funnel."

Illustrious was struck by two 550-lb and
four 1,100-lb bombs in under 10 minutes,
and but for her armoured flight deck she
would most likely have suffered the same
fate as many American and British
aircraft-carriers in the Far East. Nevertheless she was badly damaged; her
steering-gear was out of action and she
had to steer with her propellers. Admiral
Cunningham therefore ordered her to
return to Malta for repairs.

On its return voyage the following day
Cunningham's force was again attacked
by the dive-bombers of X *Fliegerkorps*.
The luckless *Southampton* was disabled
and set on fire; she had to be abandoned
by her crew and was sunk by torpedoes.

At Malta, workers and engineers
laboured frantically to get *Illustrious*
ready for action again. But on January 16
she received more damage from German
bombs, which was patched up after a
fashion. On the night of January 23
Illustrious left the Grand Harbour and
returned to Alexandria, making the remarkable speed of 28 knots. Nevertheless,
she had to be completely overhauled and
set out on a long voyage to the American
yards at Norfolk, Virginia, which undertook the work with the sympathetic
agreement of President Roosevelt.

In the absence of *Illustrious* the Admiralty decided that the carrier *Formidable*, which was in the Atlantic, should
proceed to Alexandria round the Cape of
Good Hope. Without fleet air cover,
Admiral Cunningham was unable to take
any action in the waters south of Sicily
until *Formidable* joined his flag, which
she did, in spite of the Luftwaffe's attempts
to mine the Suez Canal and the ap-
proches to Alexandria, on March 10.

Meanwhile the German bombers based
in Sicily kept Malta under constant air
bombardment. Heavy losses were inflicted
on the island's aircraft, which were under

the command of Air Vice-Marshal H. P. Lloyd. At the end of February the surviving Wellington bombers had to be brought back to Egypt; the fighters had been suffering similar losses, and on March 11 the Hurricanes, the only aircraft on Malta capable of tackling the Messerschmitt 109's and 110's on anything like equal terms, were reduced to eight battleworthy machines.

From March 1941, however, the need for air support for the Afrika Korps and for Operation "Marita" in the Balkans compelled General Geissler to divert a large number of his squadrons to these new operational theatres. The inevitable result was a slackening of the pressure put on Malta by X *Fliegerkorps*. Between April 3 and May 21 Force H was able to supply Malta with 82 Hurricanes, flown from the carriers *Ark Royal* and *Furious*.

Rome and Berlin reinforce North Africa

It is true that the German High Command and the Italian *Comando Supremo* failed to take full advantage of the temporary local superiority in all neighbouring waters achieved by the transfer of X *Fliegerkorps* to Sicily. Nevertheless, the actions of X *Fliegerkorps* gave the Axis three months in which to transfer troops to North Africa for the defence of Tripolitania against the British, which was done with very little loss. From this point of view, the air and sea engagements between Sicily and Tunisia on January 10–11 had much more serious consequences than the destruction of the *Southampton* and the temporary disablement of the *Illustrious*.

Between February 1 and June 30, 1941, no less than 81,785 Axis troops were landed at Tripoli with approximately 450,000 tons of weapons, fuel, and ammunition. In February and March, with the temporary neutralisation of Malta, the troops were shipped with very few casualties. These increased slightly from April onwards, but until June 30 casualties totalled only 4.8 per cent of all the troops embarked.

First to arrive were the Italian "Ariete" and "Trento" Divisions, together with the German 5th Light Division, which was the first contingent of the *Deutsches Afrika Korps* or D.A.K.

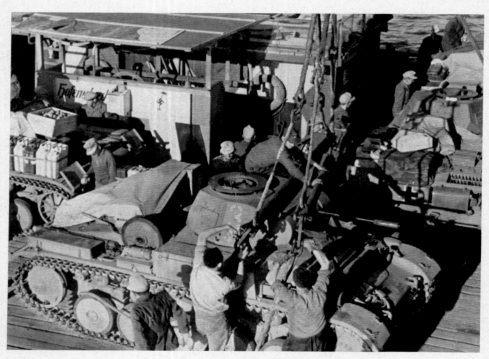

△ ◁ Two curious British soldiers inspect a portrait of the "war-lord" Mussolini, whose armies they had just defeated.
△ ▷ The spoils of war lined up for inspection. At Benghazi alone, the Italians had abandoned 112 tanks, 216 guns, and 1,500 vehicles. Even if their morale had not been completely broken, the Italians had lost so much matériel in their precipitate retreat that they would have been unable to launch a counter-offensive. △ Advent of the new order: tanks of the German 5th Light Division are unloaded from an Italian ship.

Rommel arrives in Tripoli

On February 6, 1941, Lieutenant-General Erwin Rommel was received by Brauchitsch, who gave him instructions for his new mission. He was appointed to command the expeditionary corps which was to be sent to Africa, and received orders to proceed to Africa as soon as possible. Rommel's intention, as he noted in his diary, was to examine the possibilities of using the new formation. It was anticipated that the first German troops would

arrive in mid-February and that the last unit of the 5th Light Division would be landed in mid-April. By the end of May the last detachments of the 15th Panzer Division should be in position, and the D.A.K. ready to move.

In his new rôle Rommel was to take his orders from Marshal Graziani. This was decided only after O.K.W. and *Comando Supremo* had agreed that the original plan for a close defence of Tripoli should be abandoned. The Italian and German forces, under Rommel's immediate command, would move further down the Gulf of Sirte and base their defence of Tripoli on Buerat. Rommel was authorised to appeal to the German Army High Command over Graziani's head, if the latter's orders looked like endangering the safety of the expeditionary force or the honour of the German Army.

In the afternoon of the same day, Hitler received Rommel and told him that he would be accompanied to Africa by Colonel Schmundt, the Führer's personal aide-de-camp. On February 11, Rommel presented himself to General Guzzoni, acting Chief of the General Staff in the absence of General Cavallero at the Albanian front. After a quick review of the situation with General Roatta, Italian Army Chief-of-Staff, Rommel set off for North Africa via Catania, where he conferred with Geissler. On February 12 he arrived at Tripoli and reported to General Gariboldi, who had just relieved Graziani.

And thus this remarkable commander began his military career in Africa.

The British Light Tank Mark VI

Weight: 5.2 tons.
Crew: 3.
Armament: one .5-inch Vickers machine gun with 400 rounds, and one .303-inch Vickers machine gun with 2,500 rounds.
Armour: 15-mm maximum, 4-mm minimum.
Engine: Meadows 6-cylinder inline, 88-hp.
Speed: 35 mph maximum.
Range: 125 miles.
Length: 13 feet 2 inches.
Width: 6 feet 10 inches.
Height: 7 feet 5 inches.

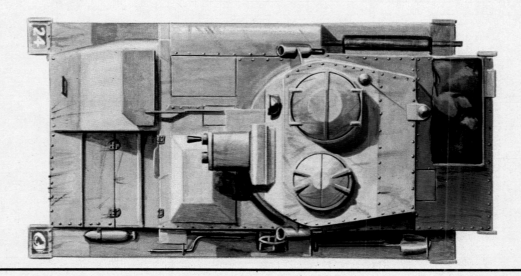

1939

January
11–13. Chamberlain and Halifax visit Mussolini.
26. Proclamation of Franco-British solidarity.

March
14. Slovakia proclaims independence.
15. German troops enter Prague, and take over Bohemia and Moravia.
16. Hitler declares that "Czechoslovakia has ceased to exist."
17. Britain and France protest against the violation of the Munich Agreement.
31. Britain gives Poland her guarantee of support.

April
6–7. Mussolini's ultimatum to Albania is followed by occupation.
13. French agreement to assist Greece and Rumania.
17. Diplomatic talks begin between Germany and the Soviet Union.
28. Conscription voted in by the British Parliament. Hitler cancels the Anglo-German Naval Agreement of 1935 and the Polish-German Non-Aggression Treaty of 1934.

May
3. Molotov replaces Litvinov.
22. The Pact of Steel.
23. Hitler plans the invasion of Poland.

July
3. The R.A.F. flies in France.

August
11–12. Discussions between Hitler, Ribbentrop, and Ciano.
11. Allied mission visits Moscow.
14. Hitler holds a conference with his generals.
20. Letter from Hitler to Stalin requesting a meeting.
22. New military conference at Berchtesgaden.
23. Russo-German Pact signed in Moscow. The Pact includes a secret protocol which divides eastern Europe between Germany and the Soviet Union.
25. German offensive on Poland postponed.
Anglo-Polish treaty of mutual assistance.
31. Hitler gives the order for the attack on Poland.

September
1. Invasion of Poland. At 0445 hours German troops attack without warning. France and Britain mobilise.
3. War declared by France and Britain after Hitler has ignored

their ultimatum.
4–12. French "Saar Offensive" fails to relieve the pressure on Poland.
10–17. Battle of the Bzura. Desperately hard fighting between the trapped Poles and 8th Army.
17. Russian and German troops meet in Poland.
18. *Courageous* sunk in the Bristol Channel.
26. Formation of a Polish Government in London and Paris. Luftwaffe attacks the fleet in Scapa Flow.
28. Surrender of Warsaw. Russo-German Treaty of Delimitation partitions Poland. Russia declares non-aggression pact with the Baltic States.

October
14. Russia gives ultimatum to Finland.
Royal Oak sunk in Scapa Flow.
29. Conference between Hitler and the general staff on the campaign in the West.

November
8. A bomb attempt on Hitler's life in Munich.
30. Red Army invades Finland; Marshal Mannerheim commands the Finnish defence.

December
13. Battle of the River Plate. Scuttling of the *Graf Spee* at Montivideo.

1940

January
5. Britain's Minister of War, Mr. Hore Belisha, is dismissed. Oliver Stanley replaces him.
8. Butter, bacon, and sugar are rationed in Britain.
12. German officer captured in Belgium carrying plans of the proposed invasion of northern France.

February
10. The Russians break through the Mannerheim Line at Summa. Finland's position becomes impossible.
14. Britain announces the arming of merchant ships in the North Sea.
16. The "*Altmark* incident" in Norway.
17. Britain makes plans to evacuate 400,000 school children to rural areas.

March
12. Finno-Soviet peace treaty.
21. Paris, Reynaud's cabinet succeeds Daladier.
28. Britain and France agree not to declare a separate peace.

April
8–9. Germany attacks Norway. Landings at Tromsö, occupation of

Narvik, Bergen, and Oslo. The Royal Navy lays mines in Norwegian waters.
9. Occupation of Denmark.
9–10. The Allies declare their intention of defending Norway.
10. British naval victory at Narvik.

May

1. Allied evacuation of Namsos.
10. German invasion of Belgium, Holland, Luxembourg, and France. Fall of Maastricht and Malmédy. Churchill succeeds Chamberlain.
13. Liège falls, the Germans cross the Meuse at Dinant and Sedan. Queen Wilhelmina arrives in Britain. Churchill makes his famous "Blood and toil" speech.
14. The fall of Rotterdam and capitulation of the Dutch army.
15. Panzer offensive west of the Meuse. General Giraud replaces Corap.
17. The Germans reach the Oise.
18. Pétain becomes Vice-President, Antwerp falls, and the Germans cross the Somme.

19. General Giraud taken prisoner. Weygand recalled to take command of the French Army.
20. The Germans reach Laon, Cambrai, Arras, Amiens, and Abbeville.
21. General Blanchard succeeds Billotte.
22. Weygand presents his counter-attack plan.
26. Operation "Dynamo", the evacuation of the Dunkirk bridgehead, begins.
28. Léopold III and the Belgian Army capitulate.

29–31. Lille falls. The Dunkirk evacuation continues.

June

3. Dunkirk falls.

5. General de Gaulle becomes Under-Secretary of State for War in Reynaud's cabinet.
The Germans launch their major offensive against France, the beginning of the Battle of the Somme.
7. The Germans reach Montdidier, Forges-les-Eaux, and Noyon. The King of Norway leaves for Britain and the Norwegian Army capitulates.
9. Dieppe, Rouen, and Compiègne fall and the Germans push towards Dijon.
10. Mussolini declares war on France.
10–11. The Germans cross the Seine and the Marne. The Maginot Line is abandoned and a general withdrawal on the Loire follows.
The Government evacuates Paris and moves to Tours.
14. The French Government moves to Bordeaux.
Paris declared an open city as the Germans enter.
15. Weygand refuses to surrender the French Army.
16. Franco-British union rejected. Pétain's Government succeeds Reynaud's.
17–18. The Germans reach the Swiss frontier and attack the Army of the Alps in the rear.
17. The French ask for armistice terms. Pétain broadcasts to the French to "stop fighting".
18. De Gaulle's appeal to continue the fight in a broadcast from London.
20. Admiral Darlan gives the secret order for the French fleet to be scuttled if the Germans attempt to capture it.
The Italians take the offensive on the Alpine front.

22. Armistice signed at Rethondes. In the east the 3rd, 5th, and 8th French Armies—a total of 400,000 men—surrender.
24. The Franco-Italian armistice signed in Rome.
25. Fighting stops on all fronts.
27. Pierre Laval elected Vice-President of the Council of Ministers.
28. Marshal Balbo shot down by Italian A.A. fire over Libya. Great Britain recognises General de Gaulle as the leader of the Free French. Channel Islands evacuated of all military personnel and many civilians.

July

1. The Germans occupy Jersey and Guernsey.
2–3. Government set up at Vichy.
3. British attack the French fleet at Mers el Kébir and seize French ships in British ports.
3–4. Vichy and London break off diplomatic relations.
5. New Rumanian Government announces its friendship with the Axis Powers.
7. Naval agreement at Alexandria between Cunningham and Godfroy.
8. The British attack the *Richelieu* at Dakar.
9. Battle of Cape Spartivento between British and Italian naval forces.
10. The National Assembly gives Pétain full governmental authority. The Battle of Britain begins.
19. Hitler offers Britain a "last appeal to reason."
21. Czechoslovak government-in-exile set up in London; recognised by Britain on the 23rd.
22. Halifax refuses Hitler's offer.
26–28. Rumania accedes to Russia's ultimatum on Bessarabia.

August

1. Italy attacks British Somaliland.
1–20. Luftwaffe attacks British ports.
2. De Gaulle condemned to death in his absence by the Vichy Government.
7. Agreement between Churchill and de Gaulle on the formation of Free French Forces.
13. "Eagle Day": the Luftwaffe launches 1,485 sorties. The Germans lose 45 aircraft and the R.A.F. 13.
15. In 1,790 sorties the Germans lose 75 aircraft to the R.A.F.'s 34. The Greek cruiser *Helle* is torpedoed and sunk; the Italians are strongly suspected.
23. All-night German raid signals the beginning of the "London Blitz".
25. The R.A.F. conducts its first raid on Berlin.
26–28. French Equatorial Africa joins de Gaulle.
29. Rumania cedes most of Transylvania to Hungary.

September

3. Fifty American destroyers transferred to Britain.
5. Japanese offensive in Indo-China.
7. The first major air raid on London.
13. The Italian offensive begins in North Africa.
15. Massive air attack on London.
16. Sidi Barrani taken by the Italians.

17. Hitler postpones Operation "Sea Lion" until further notice.
23–25. Defeat of the Free French and British at Dakar.
27. Tripartite Pact between Japan, Italy, and Germany.
30. Serrano Suñer visits Rome.

October

3. Bessarabia annexed by Russia.
4. Hitler and Mussolini meet at the Brenner Pass.
7. German troops enter Rumania.
12. Hitler postpones the invasion of Britain until spring 1941.
15. Italian War Council decides on the attack on Greece.
23. Hitler and Franco meet.

24. Talks between Hitler and Pétain at Montoire.
28. Following the refusal of their ultimatum the Italians attack Greece.
The British promise help to the Greeks.
Hitler and Mussolini meet at Florence.
31. The British occupy Canea in Crete.

November

1. Italians reach the Kalamas river in Greece.
3. Greek Evzone regiments trap the 3rd Alpine Div. and take 5,000 prisoners.
4. Roosevelt re-elected President of the United States.
11. British air attack on the Italian fleet at Taranto.

20–24. Hungary, Rumania and Slovakia join the Tripartite Pact.
22. Greek victory at Koritsa.
29. German High Command issues draft plan for "Barbarossa".

December

6. Cavallero replaces Badoglio.
9. Operation "Compass", Wavell's offensive against the Italians in Libya.
12. Sidi Barrani taken by the British.
Italians retreat in Albania.
16. Roosevelt introduces "Lend-Lease".
Sollum taken by the British.
29. London bombed by the Luftwaffe.

1941

January

3. Attack on Bardia. X *Fliegerkorps* arrives in Italy.
5. General Annibale Bergonzoli surrenders the XXIII Corps with 45,000 prisoners.
10. X *Fliegerkorps*, based in Sicily, attacks the aircraft-carrier *Illustrious*.
14. Conference at Athens, General Wavell and Air Chief-Marshal Longmore meet General Metaxas, King George II of the Hellenes, and General Papagos.
21. British attack Tobruk.
22. General Pitassi Mannella surrenders, and with him go 25,000 prisoners.
24. Australians and British attack the Italian position at Derna.

February

5. British reach Beda Fomm and cut off the Italian line of retreat.
6. Benghazi captured.
7. 20,000 Italians surrender with Generals Cona and Babini.
The British capture 1,500 vehicles at Beda Fomm.
10. Marshal Graziani hands over his command to General Gariboldi.
12. Lieutenant-General Rommel arrives in Tripoli.